SCOTTISH
RUGBY UNION

THE OFFICIAL SRU ANNUAL 1992-1993

SCOTTISH
RUGBY UNION

THE OFFICIAL
SCOTTISH RUGBY UNION ANNUAL 1992-1993

Edited by Ian McLauchlan

MAINSTREAM
PUBLISHING

in association with

The Royal Bank of Scotland

The photographs in this book have been reproduced with the kind permission of  THE SCOTSMAN

First published in Great Britain in 1992 by
MAINSTREAM PUBLISHING COMPANY (EDINBURGH) LTD
7 Albany Street
Edinburgh EH1 3UG

ISBN 1 85158 484 6

A catalogue record for this book is available from the British Library

Typeset in Garamond by Saxon Printing Ltd, Derby

Printed in Great Britain by Butler & Tanner Ltd, Frome

CONTENTS

FOREWORD

From Armchair to Touchline, a Fine Tradition to Cherish

Ten years ago, The Royal Bank of Scotland became the first sponsor of an international rugby match.

Since then, all Scotland's games at Murrayfield have been Royal Bank internationals and we have injected more than £2 million into grass roots rugby through our good friends at the SRU.

In return, Scotland's rugby players have said 'thank you' in the biggest and best way imaginable. They won two Grand Slams in a decade when there had been only one in the previous hundred years. Both of those reached a climax in a head-to-head at Murrayfield – two out of only four winner-takes-all encounters in rugby history!

No sponsor could have asked for more – and along the way we saw, in the matches against our traditional 'neighbours' in the Five Nations Championship, against our long-running Commonwealth rivals and against the exciting newcomers, some of the very best confrontations of modern rugby.

We at The Royal Bank of Scotland have always sought to build on our showcase sponsorship. Commissioning the Ronnie Browne paintings *The Turning Point 1984* and *Underdog Rampant 1990*, exhibiting them around Scotland, funding team posters and calendars – all of these initiatives have, we believe, helped Scots savour some of the finest moments in this great game.

The support for this imaginative new venture, *The Official Scottish Rugby Union Annual*, stems from the same conviction – that we have a fine tradition of rugby football which deserves to be cherished from the armchair as much as from the touchline.

Dr George Mathewson
Chief Executive
The Royal Bank of Scotland

PREFACE

Robin Charters

President, Scottish Rugby Union

IT GIVES me great pleasure to write the preface to this, the first *Official Scottish Rugby Annual*. I trust that this will be the start of a long series of books – there is, I am sure, a market for this type of publication and the more we publicise our game the more likely we will be to attract youngsters to take it up.

I am delighted to see The Royal Bank of Scotland giving their support to the book because their association with the Scottish Rugby Union has been a close and friendly one. Some of us can hardly believe that it is ten years since the Royal Bank began their sponsorship of internationals at Murrayfield: the first game was against Fiji on 25 September 1982. I hope there will be many more.

Talk of Murrayfield leads me on naturally to the redevelopment of the national stadium. Quite simply, the SRU are determined to make this one of the finest sporting venues in Europe. The work on the new seated accommodation at both ends of the ground is coming on apace and should be complete by the end of this year. As you may know, the Union has decided to rebuild completely the West Stand which, when finished, will provide modern standards of comfort and safety for all spectators.

We ask you to bear with us during the period of reconstruction. Until we reach full capacity – and probably after that as well – satisfying the demand for international tickets will be difficult. The SRU, and the players who pull on the blue jersey, are very grateful for the enthusiastic support of the Scottish public which I believe has played a part in our recent success on the field.

The game, of course, cannot stand still. This season we will be operating under a radical change in the laws which has been introduced with the intention of making rugby more attractive to watch and play. There should be fewer stoppages for minor infringements and, hopefully, a greater incentive for teams to go for more tries. But it will take time for players to get used to the new laws and we should not be too impatient in looking for the benefits.

The Scottish Rugby Union is only too well aware that we must market our game; we live in a very competitive world where young people have an ever-expanding choice of how to spend their leisure time. We remain convinced, however, that rugby is a most satisfying, rewarding and enjoyable activity which breaks down many barriers.

I hope that this proves to be a successful season, and that our international side can keep up the excellent work of recent years. Most of all I hope that at the end of it, there will be more people involved in the game at all levels. How about you?

Murrayfield
August 1992

THE DOMESTIC SEASON

LOOKING BACK

Memorable Moments from Last Season

Brian Meek

IT WAS an evil day at the end of February, the wind whipping off the Teviot and straight down the field at Mansfield Park, stinging rain bit into the faces of the players as they completed their warm-up. In the passage under the grandstand I was talking to one of the legends of the game, a man who had graced this venue for many years. Jim Renwick was far from happy, his beloved Hawick, rulers of all they surveyed when he was at his peak, were in relegation trouble – an almost unheard of phenomenon.

The game they were about to play was against Watsonians. Gavin, Scott, Roger Baird, Andrew Ker, Stuart Johnston, et al., and the Greens were desperate for the points. But how, I posed to Renwick, had the great old club come to this parlous state? Where had all the good players gone? He ran his hand across his now quite sparse scalp. That gesture brought back so many memories: he would do it on the field, in the heat of an

international, and you knew he was planning some special magic. Now his smile was a little tired. 'There are just not as many laddies playing the game. If there was one hundred of them in my day there are only sixty now. And there is no work for them here when they leave the school. These are hard times in Hawick but we will come through them.' I pressed him a little further. Would it not be to the club's advantage to do what many of their rivals have opted for and simply go out and recruit the players they need from anywhere? From New Zealand, or Australia or South Africa? Renwick was absolutely firm: 'I am no' fur that. This is the town's club and we will get out of trouble by standing the gither, no' by looking for outside help. Mind you, that's only my opinion – I'm no' criticising clubs that have done it.' No, he wouldn't, that was never his style.

So, his town still needed him, and Jim Renwick was back at Mansfield to help to

The Great Escape. Melrose v Edinburgh Accies (The Scotsman)

coach the backs. The game which followed will not go down in history as a classic but there were splendid examples of courage on both sides. Baird reminded us what a class player he has been by scoring the only try after Gav had come into the line like a howitzer. Ker dropped a goal and Hawick were 9–0 down before David Gray kicked an important penalty before the break. Now with the gale at their backs and their loyal supporters howling them on, Hawick piled on the pressure. Two dropped-goals, one by Gray, the other by Scott Welsh brought the score to level. But the Watsonian defence held firm and there were no further breaches.

Back in the tunnel Renwick was half-pleased, half-frustrated. 'They gave all they had – you can't ask for more than that. We needed both points though – now we are going to have to beat Gala at Netherdale.' Rugby's 'old firm' were to be pitted against one another in one of the most important games in the long series between the two.

Well I recall the 1977 play-off when Gala and the Greens took part in the only play-off we have ever had for the First Division title. Hawick won that day; this time they had to do so to try and save their spot in the top rank. You could feel the tension as the teams took the field. A few of the great Hawick names of the past, Norman Suddon, Brian Hegarty and of course, Renwick, gathered to shout them on. As a game it was a bomber; there were more errors than in the dunce's examination paper and hardly a back movement worth the name. But as a dramatic, gripping event it sent the pulses racing. Welsh kicked Hawick ahead with two penalties but Michael Dods – brother Peter

was on the sick list – used the wind to good effect and squared the account. Jim Hay, the Hawick hooker, set up the vital try. He had already done sterling work with a couple of strikes against the head. This time he chuntered off on a charge, scattering opponents on his way. When the time came to release the pass, there was Alan Tomes to take it and barge over. Who? Alan Tomes. Not the Alan Tomes that played in the 1974 Hawick Championship-winning side, not the former Scotland and British Lions lock, why he must be forty if he is a day? That's absolutely correct; that is the man and that is his age and, just for good measure, he is still travelling from the North of England every week to give Hawick his services.

I went into the Greens' dressing room which, as you can imagine, was buzzing like the Mardi Gras. The big man was removing his sweat band; he looked tired but enormously happy. 'I don't score too many tries,' he admitted, 'but that one was very sweet.' He reminded me that he had come into the Hawick team when he was 18 and had been playing English county rugby before that. But why is he still there, what is the motivation of playing with the lads who could be his sons? 'Days like today. I found the last ten minutes pretty hard but I thoroughly enjoyed the game.' Nor would he even admit to retiring. 'I never make these decisions at the end of a season. We will wait until the summer is over and see how I feel.' This guy could be the Stanley Matthews of rugby at this rate. The debt owed to him by Hawick can never be repaid: we should remember that the great servants of our game hold to the amateur ethic above all, they play for fun.

This chapter was supposed to be a reflection on the teams gone by. I have to tell you that, as seasons go, I did not think the 1991-92 was any kind of classic. Perhaps after the thrill of the World Cup, we found it a little difficult to go back to 'auld claes an' parrich'. But I shall always recall Renwick and Tomes and the part they played in warming the cockles of this observer's heart.

Let me tell of another happy, if lachrymose, day which will not be easily forgotten. At the end of March I was posted to Peebles where Dundee HSFP were set to clinch their place in the First Division, a truly marvellous performance which owed much to the influence of former Scotland captain, David Leslie. On the way to the match my windscreen wipers were working overtime; by the time I had arrived it was tipping down. I remember Peebles well, having played there on many occasions. The trick was, if you were a penalty goal ahead and feeling the pressure, to boot the ball into the river. On this important day it looked as though the river had moved onto the pitch.

Keith Robertson, winger turned scribe, and I waded across to a tiny shelter on the far side. There we were joined by Andy Nicol's mother, his grandfather and sundry worthies all of whom had come to throw their bonnets in the air. The only problem was that we could not see all that well. I will spare you the details of how difficult it is to report a match when your pad is soaking through, none of your pens will write, and the players' numbers have all disappeared in the glaur. Indeed it was extremely hard to distinguish even one team from another. Nicol, having a truly golden season, I could still spot because he

appeared to be everywhere and Derek Milne had a great game at no. 8, scoring a precious try. Peebles competed right to the end and the scoreline of 15–4 in Dundee's favour was a little hard on them. Still you had to be happy for the Dundonians knowing how far they had come.

Leslie, of course, was not going around handing out lollipops. 'That was a dreadful performance. Just wait until I see them at training on Tuesday.' The man never changes. In the dressing-room Nicol, looking like a dead ringer for Al Jolson, put it a bit more tactfully. 'I know it was not very pretty but there are times when you have to keep it tight.'

The aforementioned Robertson was so overcome by the emotion of the occasion that he bought me a cup of tea. I was still reeling from this shock when I discovered I had lost my car keys; that awful, 'where am I going to find a garage on a Saturday afternoon' feeling hit the pit of my stomach. Having tramped out on the sodden field and searched without success I returned to the vehicle. The keys were where I had left them, in the lock of the front door; civilised place Peebles!

What else did I enjoy last season? Going to Currie. There is definitely something quite special about the atmosphere at Malleny Park which appears to give rise to the most dramatic matches and colourful characters. At one time a local supporter used to have a suit in the Currie colours, one leg a different shade to the other: he is dressed more soberly these days but you will still meet more than your fair share of eccentrics. A lot of them will be on the field.

Graham Hogg, the Currie coach, explains that his side has to play running rugby because 'we simply do not have big forwards'. That is true but his side does contain some excellent grafters in the pack, Duncan Wilson, Adam Elms and Peter Farrar among them. The backs are marshalled by Ally Donaldson and how good it was to see this talented fly-half receive representative recognition last season. Among his troops are David Beggy, everyone's idea of what an Irishman should be like, who can play full-back or wing and flies home to take part in Gaelic football when he needs a bit of extra stimulus. To say Beggy is unorthodox is to say Eric Morecambe was quite funny. David rises like a salmon to swallow the high ball; he scores quite outrageous tries; he also gifts quite a few to the opposition and his fag will be lit before he has run from the field to the dressing-room. The Irish selectors have had a look at Beggy. After their experience in New Zealand maybe they will give a run to the Currie player. The least he would do is cheer them up.

A typical Currie performance was against Gala in January. With ten minutes of the second half gone the home side were 25–3 in front and Gala were just longing to get back on to the bus to the Borders. Suddenly, for no discernible reason, the Currie concentration just disappeared: they conceded four tries, one of which Beggy presented to Michael Dods when he tried to chip the Gala winger and only succeeded in popping the ball straight into his arms. Donaldson finally managed to steady the ship as his penalty steered Currie home 28–25. An ashen-faced coach Hogg asked me 'what did you make of

Heriot's v Hawick (The Scotsman)

Bay of Plenty praise the Bell's (The Scotsman*)*

all that?' We shook our heads and made off for a reviver. Seriously, if you are a neutral and out looking for some excitement do take in a match at Malleny. Everyone is very friendly as well.

At Meggetland in May the final of the Castlemaine XXXX Cup brought together two Division VII rivals, Ross High and Duns. The latter had already gained promotion and added the trophy to their collection with a convincing 52–11 victory. That was not the only aspect which impressed me. Out on the Duns right wing was Sandy Thomson with whom some six years ago, I journeyed to Villefrance-sur-Saône where he played his

part in a famous Scotland B victory. What is he doing operating at this level of the game? 'Enjoying myself,' he replied. 'I was not too happy in my last seasons at Kelso but being part of this club has restored my enthusiasm for the game.' He certainly looked to be having a grand time, scoring a try and setting up another. One wonders if more players who have reached international level could contribute something, and continue to enjoy themselves, by turning out for the smaller clubs.

Duns are lucky – they do not just have Thomson; Adam Marshall, the former Kelso front-row man, is there too and his experience is proving invaluable. In the dressing-room I asked about the shoulder he had dislocated so many times. 'Yes it was ten actually,' he replied, and pointed to the pin. 'I don't have to tackle all that much these days so, as long as it lasts, I am going to keep on playing. Our job here is to keep their feet on the ground.' What a fine attitude. Former Watsonians and still Scottish Schools coach, Peter Gallagher is the guiding hand at the club. 'I live in the town – it was the 500th anniversary of Duns in 1990 so it seemed a good moment to become involved.' It seems to me a good example of the rugby community operating at its best.

In this chapter I have picked a few of my personal highlights from the domestic scene. To end I should like to tell you just a little bit about my meeting last year with Dr Danie Craven, the man who has done more than any other to keep the game alive on the African continent. We met in his office at Stellenbosch on a gorgeous morning when the university town looked at its best.

The Doc didn't look too bad either for a man of 80 who has had a heart bypass operation and was just about to have another for a broken bone in his back. He still has a fiercely competitive nature and was finding it hard to compromise with some of the new faces demanding the right to run the sport in South Africa. 'I am not going to step aside now and let all our hard work go to waste,' he insisted. It should be remembered that integration was not forced on him, he chose to take that route as far back as 1977. 'At first we tried playing white teams against the others but we soon learned it was better to play with people of different colours rather than against them. That way you share the joy of victory, the sadness of defeat.'

He is still a visionary, a man who believes the game will have to change even more fundamentally than most could contemplate. 'I want to see a game with only six or seven scrums and the same number of line-outs. We must learn to keep the ball alive.' If, as we all hope, the next World Cup is played in South Africa, a great debt will be owed to Danie Craven. In fact the first competition would probably not have taken place had his delegation not refrained from voting when the idea of such a tournament was proposed. 'Our instructions from home were to vote against but, when we realised how enthusiastic some people were, we decided to abstain at the International Board meeting and the proposal was carried by one vote.'

The Doc sent his best wishes to all his friends in Scotland and walked down the driveway. 'Rugby,' he insisted, 'can break down all barriers, colour, class, creed. Not even religion can do that.' In their own way, I suppose, Jim Renwick, Alan Tomes and Sandy Thomson were saying that too. It was not such a bad season after all.

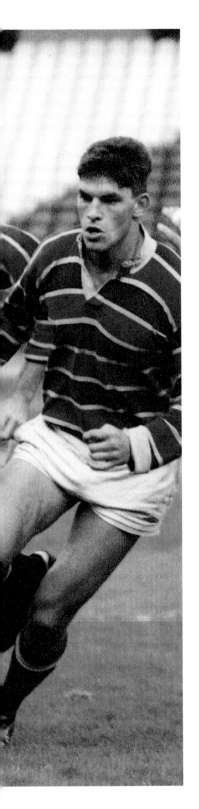

Graham Marshall outnumbered by Edinburgh Borderers
(*The* Scotsman)

The final hurdle: Melrose v GHK
(*The* Scotsman)

Entertaining Currie (The Scotsman)

The Royal Bank
of Scotland

MELROSE BACK ON TOP

The McEwan's National Leagues

George Mackay

IT WAS A funny League season. Jim Telfer was seen to smile, his austere façade split by a beam some degrees warmer than moonlight glinting on a silver coffin nameplate. But that was right at the end, when his pride of Melrose young lions wrapped up their second McEwan's Scottish Club Championship in three years, aptly at their Greenyards home with a 27–16 victory over Glasgow High-Kelvinside. Maestro coach Telfer could even justly permit himself an inward chuckle, for Melrose had started the title race fancied but not favourites. He had driven, cajoled and encouraged a richly-talented but relatively-inexperienced side to triumph, once again vindicating, if it still were needed, his unswerving belief in the virtues of total dedication to the game.

Once they had moved into the lead, a third of the way into the race, Melrose were never headed, although there was the odd wobble along the way. Three encounters virtually decided the title issue. The first was early in December when Border pride, keen rivalry and unbeaten records were all pitched into the Netherdale arena. Melrose stunned Gala with an instant blitz which swept them

into a 28–3 half-time lead as Gregor Townsend, the 18-year-old star schoolboy stand-off, learned the high price to be paid for mistakes at top club level, Craig Chalmers delighting in conducting the lesson. Gala did fight back in the second half to narrow the deficit but defeat took a heavy toll. Seemingly psychologically shattered, they went on to lose their next five games in a row. All the vast experience gleaned by Peter Dods from campaigns around the world's rugby fields could not heal the damage: Gala were a spent force as far as the Championship went. Melrose went into the Christmas break with seven straight wins and a useful three points lead but secretly feeling relieved to have reaped such handsome rewards from hitting top form only in brief patches.

'Saturday is a big game. Edinburgh Academicals have a strong side, full of big names. We will have to give it our best shot,' prophetically predicted Robbie Brown, Melrose's 23-year-old captain and lock forward, before the opening League match of the New Year. How right he was. His side came so close to toppling off their perch. Accies surged into a 15–3 first-half lead and

Another Melrose drive v Heriot's
(The Scotsman*)*

Chipper Lineen (The Scotsman)

Melrose had to draw deeply on their reserves of willpower and stamina to salvage the 15–15 draw which kept their title ambitions on course. Afterwards John Allan, the Accies captain, was in introspective mood. 'We came down to take on the League leaders in their own backyard and we got a draw. We should be satisfied,' he said. 'But we're devastated. We know we blew it.' The Raeburn Place club in, as it later turned out, the last season of Scotland front row col-

leagues David Sole and John Allan, went on to earn solid respect for doggedly battling on in a cause they suspected in their hearts to be lost, and finished the race respectable runners-up. Melrose went on to glory.

They confirmed their championship potential in the most decisive manner with a glorious, five-try, 32–6 victory over their only remaining serious challengers, Heriot's, at Goldenacre. For the first time the Green-yards backs cut loose, weaving intricate

Terrible Twins, Jim and Fin (The Scotsman*)*

patterns at high speed to confuse and confound their pedestrian opponents. Like Gala before them, Heriot's never regained their appetite after the experience.

Under Telfer's astute guidance, Melrose's triumph was essentially a collective effort, with vital contributions coming from all areas. Robbie Brown, showing maturity beyond his years, gave a solid lead, Euan Simpson proved a valuable recruit alongside the captain, and big Doddie Weir,

released from the grind of second row, took to the wider horizons of no. 8 with a flair and energy which inspired judges of the stature of John Beattie, no mean performer in the role, and Telfer himself to suggest the 21-year-old's international future could lie in the back row.

The three Redpath brothers, Andy (Ripper), Bryan and Craig, regaining ground lost in the previous season, all played their distinctively varied parts and Craig Chalmers

The best of enemies. Gary Armstrong evades Craig Chalmers (The Scotsman*)*

orchestrated operations with such impressive authority as to draw the admiring comment from Brown that 'Craig is an even better player after the World Cup. He has been tremendous'.

But Melrose's discovery of the season unquestionably was Gary Parker, a 5 ft 5 in firecracker who has a happy knack of succeeding at anything he turns his hand to. A schoolboy international at Galashiels Academy, he turned to soccer with such flair that he played professionally for Hearts. Soccer took him to New Zealand where in six years he 'never touched a rugby ball' – a feat akin to staying teetotal in a brewery. 'I came back to Melrose just happy to play rugby and find myself with two League winners' medals,' said the ebullient 25-year-old. Melrose, of course, also won the domestic battle they call the Border League. Parker's progress with Melrose was meteoric. A replacement for the first League game against Stewart's-Melville he came on on the wing, a position he had never played, and held his place for the rest of the season. He took over the goal-kicking from Craig Chalmers at the turn of the year and, giving the ball an almighty thump, quickly piled up an impressive 74 League points.

To Melrose went the jackpot: what of the others who lined up so hopefully for the League race? The starting gun fired late, on 9 November. After the mega-spectacle of the World Cup, with its global media spotlight and attendant hype, the McEwan's Scottish Leagues crept in almost surreptitiously, with scarcely a pause to draw breath.

It certainly caught defending champions Boroughmuir on the wrong foot. Coach Bruce Hay gave brave promise of a more expansive game. 'There is more to rugby than kicking the ball up in the air and chasing it,' he said. He may not have had in mind the pitfalls which tripped the champions up and left them languishing at the bottom of the table without a point after their first two games. Boroughmuir at least did have the later satisfaction of showing what they could achieve on the field when they eclipsed Melrose 23–10 at Meggetland, the only blot on the new champions' record. The Edinburgh club still have a rich seam of talent to mine, with Peter Wright, Stewart Reid, Grant Wilson, Graham Drummond, and Murry Walker all poised to blossom. Boroughmuir can and will come again.

One of their opening setbacks was against promoted Watsonians. The crowds once again flocked to Myreside, drawn by the glamour of the Hastings brothers, Gavin and Scott, pin-ups of the twin-set set, and ex-caps Roger Baird and Andrew Ker. For a couple of glorious, heady weeks Watsonians led the League, before cold reality set in in the form of heavyweight packs who ground down the Myreside butterfly.

Heriot's, runners-up for two seasons, again pinned their hopes of the vital breakthrough on bulk, with Andy Macdonald, 6 ft 8 in, and Alex Snow, 6 ft 7 in, twin peaks in the middle-row of a power pack spearheaded by Scotland hooker Kenny Milne. And despite a humbling setback at Gala, where they embarrassingly conceded a pushover try, they stayed in the hunt until unhorsed by Melrose.

While the title race rapidly reduced to three contenders – Melrose, Edinburgh

Accies, Heriot's – the rest of the field huddled together above the relegation drop. Midway through the season only four points covered the bottom 11 clubs.

West of Scotland, relegated then promoted in the previous two seasons, became detached despite the Stakhanovite efforts of Scotland B cap Dave Barrett, who scored 119 of their 163 points. Above them it was a real dog-eat-dog scrap.

Even the unthinkable became possible. Hawick, the proudest name in Scottish club rugby, champions ten times in 14 years, were not immune from the threat of joining the lower orders. Like a great family fallen on hard times, their plight was viewed from outside the Borders, and possibly even more within them, with a mixture of concern and barely concealed glee. But there were enough resources in the town, and the green jersey generated sufficient passion to ward off that fate. Three points from their last two games, including a win over arch-rivals Gala, ensured their survival in Division One, albeit on a shaky and undignified toehold.

The unlucky losers were Stewart's-Melville – unlucky in that they scraped together ten points, the same tally as GHK and Hawick, and lost out only on points differential. Even the presence of Finlay Calder, pointed like an old war horse once more towards the gunfire, could not save them. It signalled the end of an era at Inverleith, where once the ranks were packed with Calders, Brewsters and Scotts, but Stewart's Melville have a new crop of promising youngsters such as Graeme Burns, Murray Thomson, Alex Kittle and Kenny Milligan and a season to bring them on in the less intense atmosphere of the Second Division should bear fruit.

It certainly did no harm at all to Kelso. Champions in 88 and 89, relegated last year, they bounced straight back up, winning all their 13 games. Inevitably the driving force was John Jeffrey who, bowing off the international stage, devoted his surging energies to the Poynder Park cause. Thirteen tries measured the White Shark's commitment to promotion. Kelso's prospects in the top flight next season could hang in large measure on Jeffrey's appetite and his knees remaining unimpaired. The Second Division was a two horse race whose finishing order was established on the first outing, when Kelso 'old soldiered' Dundee HSFP, the only blemish on their record.

David Leslie, not the most reticent of characters, believed the Tayside club were now ready to fulfil their destiny, a final season in Division Two having tuned the players physically and mentally for a greater challenge. 'I want to establish a centre of opportunity for youngsters of talent to graduate to representative rugby while staying in this area', said the fiercely proud Dundonian, mindful of his own experience. He did win the first of his 32 caps while playing for Dundee HSFP in Division Four but was put under intense pressure to move to a top club to advance his international career. He went first to West and then Gala, doing great things, including club championships, and even mightier feats for Scotland. But it still irks him that he was forced to go, and that fires his determination to build a launch pad for local players. Leslie's ambition has already paid off with the stunning success of

Andy Nicol in filling the massive hole in the Scotland side caused by Gary Armstrong's untimely knee injury. The 21-year-old scrum-half surprised the critics, and possibly even himself, by the composure with which he stepped into the international furnace and coolly stood up to the heat. Nicol is only the brightest in a constellation of young stars shining at Mayfield. His half back partner, Jon Newton, headed the top scorers with 164 League points and the club had five players in the Scotland under-21 squad. The emergence of Dundee as a centre of excellence and the continuing success of Stirling County are positive influences in expanding the game beyond the twin strongholds of the Borders and the Edinburgh-Glasgow axis. Now it is up to Aberdeen to get its act together.

There was little sign of that happening immediately in the lower divisions, each as rich in tales of triumph and tragedy as their elite counterparts. Grangemouth broke new ground by reaching Division Two, replacing Royal High, who did not enjoy success on the field to complement their sumptious new Barnton clubhouse. Highland, another former First Division power, slid farther down the slippery slope, losing out in a nerve-tingling relegation struggle and dropping to Division Four. Morgan Academy FP gave their own boost to the Dundee renaissance by topping Division Four and, with little St Boswells, earning promotion to Division Three. Langholm v St Boswells: that's a fixture next season which mirrors changing Border fortunes. Stewartry will carry the banner of the South West outposts into Division Four, joined by the new town men of Livingston. The West's fading fortunes in

McEwan's League Trophy. Happy Melrose (The Scotsman)

the top flights found no echo in Division Six, where Clydebank and Irvine earned a step up.

Finally, there were stirrings of invasion. Berwick, based half-a-dozen miles over the English border, swept all before them in their first campaign in Division Seven. They fielded a team composed in roughly equal measure of Scots and English and, explained president Peter Close, 'We even have an honorary president of each nationality to preserve harmony between the factions'. It seems to work too. Englishmen capturing a Scottish prize and no dissent – it was a funny League season.

Roy Laidlaw, Youth Development Officer (The Scotsman)

**The Royal Bank
of Scotland**

GAMES OF YOUTH

Scottish Youth Rugby

John Roxburgh

THE DEVELOPMENT OF youth rugby in Scotland arguably dates back to pre-1873 (when the Union was first formed), as the game of rugby in Scotland was introduced by various schools from which the adult game developed. From this early beginning, the spread of rugby in schools resulted in clubs being formed throughout Scotland and particularly in the most populated areas. At the outset, it was not uncommon for schoolboys to appear in international teams and since that time, schools have continuously produced players of the adult game.

Whilst the early development of the game was of a somewhat ad-hoc nature, the organised development of youth rugby is very recent and, with the exception of the South District, dates back to 1974. In 1974, the game of mini rugby was launched in Scotland adopting a game structure which had been developed by a working party appointed by the Union to produce a game suitable for primary schoolboys. The game of mini rugby unfortunately did not develop in primary schools as was intended and this was due to various factors, not least the predominance of lady teachers and the problem of mixed classes. Fortunately, however, the game was adopted by clubs and has

proved to be an enjoyable and productive introduction to rugby football. The game caught on rapidly and within two or three seasons over fifty clubs throughout the country were offering mini rugby, usually on a Sunday, and inter-club fixtures and tournaments were soon a regular feature of the mini rugby circuit. The progress of mini rugby was encouraged and monitored by the Union through the Technical Administrator, John Roxburgh, whose appointment coincided with the launch of the game. It soon became evident that many boys, who enjoyed mini rugby through the auspices of the club, were being lost to the game if they attended a secondary school which made no rugby provisions. In view of this, clubs were encouraged by the Union to provide facilities for these youngsters and from this what we now know as midi rugby has emerged. Midi rugby is organised in a similar way to mini rugby, principally due to the fact that club facilities are invariably fully utilised on a Saturday and any additional provisions have to take place on a Sunday.

The development of mini rugby has been of an informal nature but has been overseen and encouraged both practically and financially by the Union and is now a most important part of our rugby structure. The existence of this structure at club level was a critical factor in maintaining the game throughout and beyond the Teachers' Dispute of the early eighties and is seen now as an integral part of our development structure.

In 1991-92 season a Staged Development Programme was introduced whereby boys can progress in easy stages from mini rugby to midi rugby and subsequently to youth and adult rugby. Within the Staged Development Programme, the players experience 8, 10, 13, and 15-a-side rugby with various modifications to the laws of the game designed to promote an exciting, skilful mode of play. The provision of a continuous playing structure for youngsters was completed by the introduction of The Royal Bank Youth Leagues in season 1980-81, whereby under-18 Leagues were introduced in Edinburgh, Glasgow and the Midlands on similar lines to the long established (1920-21) Semi-Junior League in the South District. This youth league structure was of a formal nature and now includes a North League, an Inter-District Championship, and, since 1981-82, international fixtures. The emergence of a representative structure from the club under-18 scene is in parallel with the district and international structure of the Scottish schools and this parallel structure is the bottom rung of the representative ladder for the ambitious player.

In order to support all the developments at club level, and to provide much-needed player development and adult coach education, more full-time staff have been employed by the Union to support the Technical Administrator and his assistant, Douglas Arneil, who was appointed in 1980. The first such position was the appointment in 1986 of a Youth Development Officer for the Glasgow District. Since then, a further five youth development officers have been appointed to cover Edinburgh, the South, South Grampian and Angus, the South West, and North Grampian, Highlands and Islands, and the Assistant Technical Administrator undertakes such duties in the Midlands. The expansion of the youth development service is essential to provide the necessary back-up to club and school provisions for rugby football and although there is a slight improvement in the school situation, it is generally accepted that youth development at club level will remain an essential part of our structure.

The introduction of youth development officers has been recognised by other sports and by the Sports Council, and has been used as an example for sports development generally and for team sport in particular. In this context, the Sports Council, through their Team Sport Scotland programme, have appointed a Rugby Co-ordinator who works closely with the development staff of the Union and is responsible for youth development in West Lothian, together with other development projects.

One of the major problems affecting the development of youth rugby at club level is the lack of knowledgeable adult support and a major part of the annual provision comprises coaching courses at the various levels of youth rugby. In addition to the much needed coaching expertise, every club involved in youth rugby requires additional

Scottish Students v Under-21 XV (The Scotsman)

It must be his year: Shade Munro
(The Scotsman)

The long-term objectives of the programme are to have every Saturday-playing club involved in youth development and ultimately for this provision to be on an all-through basis from mini to midi to youth to adult rugby. Many clubs already have such a provision and some, such as Stirling County and Melrose are clearly reaping the benefit of providing for their own future by encouraging local youngsters. Further provisions are now being made at a more local level and Clarkston RFC have appointed their own Youth Development Officer to provide a programme whereby rugby can develop within their own catchment area and a jointly funded position is being financed by Perth and Kinross Recreational Facilities and the SRU. Two further joint funding positions are presently under discussion and the Union hopes that they will be advertised shortly.

Whilst all the support given by the SRU to the development of youth rugby is essential, it is imperative that clubs appreciate the need to develop their own youth sections in order to ensure a continuous supply of players for their adult sides.

adult recources to assist with the various administrative aspects which, in view of the age group involved, are most demanding.

The Royal Bank of Scotland

SCHOOLS OF HARD KNOCKS

The Scottish Schools Rugby Union Celebrates its Silver Jubilee

Rob Moffat

LAST SEASON (1991-92) saw the Scottish Schools Rugby Union celebrate their silver jubilee. On the schools international front it also saw Scotland under-18s defeat France for the first time, in a match that was switched from Netherdale to Murrayfield due to snow – the only other occasion that the Scots have achieved any success in this fixture was a 12–12 draw in 1988. The Scots' victory was due to a great effort by forwards against, as always, a much heavier French pack – the Lorre side almost gained 50 per cent of first phase possession – and magnificent defence by the back row and midfield. Unfortunately, after this win the Scots could not build and improve. In fact they lost their remaining four matches against Wales, Scottish Youth under-18, Ireland and England.

At this level Scotland have had few successes over the years. One major reason for the poor record in terms of results is size – an example this year, which was by no means rare or unusual, saw a prop giving away four stones to his opposite number. As a country we do not breed big players but we must try to find big forwards and work hard to make

them into good players. Perhaps the other main reason for the poor results is the level of rugby our boys are playing at school and district which is certainly not as high as in other countries. Yet the situation is not all gloom and doom as this season, as ever, there were talented individuals who have the ability to make an impact in the future such as scrum-half Ian Brydie (Dollar Academy), stand-off Duncan Hodge (Merchiston), centre Craig Joiner (Merchiston) who also played for Scotland under-19s this season, full-back/centre Cammy Murray (Knox Academy) and prop Andrew Binnie (Heriot's). The team worked hard throughout the season under the excellent captaincy of David Thomson (Hutchesons GS) and it is to be hoped that the boys involved at this level now see what is required at the top grade and will work hard to achieve this for the benefit of Scottish rugby.

Looking to next season, prospective candidates at international level have the bonus of a tour, possibly to South Africa, to look forward to. The Schools Union undoubtedly see the benefits of a tour when

Scottish Under-18 v Scottish Schools
(*The* Scotsman)

boys can train and play together at a consistently high level for four to five weeks. The benefits of the tour to New Zealand in 1988 are already in evidence with Doddy Weir, Graham Shiel and Andy Nicol already being capped from that squad and many of the others working their way up to representative level.

Still at under-18 level, in the district scene Midlands looked to be the strongest

side until they lost to the South, thus Edinburgh shared the Championship with the Midlands. The President's XV are not involved in the Championship and over the season they played Midlands, South and Glasgow.

The Scottish Schools Cup was won by Marr College who defeated St Aloysius 8–6 in another excellent final – the victory was the culmination of a first-class season by

Marr. St Aloysius are also to be congratulated on reaching the final maintaining their very good record in The Bank of Scotland Scottish Schools Cup. The top school side in Scotland over the season was undoubtedly Dollar Academy – coached by John Foster. They were undefeated by a school side for the first time in their history, they were the mainstay of the Midlands team, and four of their team, namely Scott Carnochan, Ian Brydie, John Taylor and John Melville, were capped at international level, while two others, Kenny Wallace and David Stewart, were on the bench. Frank Hadden's Merchiston also had a very good season maintaining the high quality of rugby they have produced over the past few years.

At under-15 level Glasgow were the strongest district, illustrating this with a 48–6 victory over the South in the final of the Bank of Scotland Knockout Cup. In the under-15 international Scotland lost to Wales in an exciting encounter at Myreside. Perhaps the highlight of the match was the place-kicking of the Welsh fly-half who would have embarrassed many club kickers such was his power and accuracy, but the Scots took a lot of credit from the match for the manner in which they attacked the Welsh. This was the last international at under-15 level as the age has been increased to under-16. Next season the Scots are not going to play Wales but look at the possibility of playing two district sides from England or Wales. The District Championship at home still remains at under-15 level with the Scottish Schools Rugby Union looking to improve the boys' preparations for international level by playing more than one match. This was the situation in the past.

It will be interesting over the next two or three seasons to see if a new format can produce an international side geared to play at this level.

During the season the Scottish Schools Rugby Union held two most successful events to celebrate its silver jubilee: a dinner chaired by president Brian Rookley at the Carlton Hotel and an under-14 tournament held at Murrayfield. The early stages of this competition, like the Scottish Schools Cup at under-18 level, were played at district level with qualifiers from each area playing in the rugby festival at Murrayfield.

In general schools rugby is in good heart with a large number of teachers and helpers giving up considerable amounts of their own time to teach the basic skills and disciplines to their charges. The Schools Rugby Union receives considerable financial assistance from the SRU and their sponsor, The Bank of Scotland who are once again involved in sponsoring Scottish schools rugby. This assistance is essential to develop young players and help to ensure that we maximise the potential of players in Scotland.

From a personal point of view I would like to see more schools enter the Cup in order to raise the level of competition and subject the boys to that necessary increase in standard of play. Also we must all continue to encourage more boys to play the game at school and encourage the teachers to teach the game. There is often negative talk of less involvement since the industrial action rather than positive encouragement to all involved in schoolboy rugby to constantly improve standards and enjoy the game.

Fly the flag (The Scotsman)

The Royal Bank
of Scotland

THE INTERNATIONAL SEASON

THE SCOTS SANG WALTZING MATILDA

The 1991 World Cup

Neil Drysdale

THE HAMADA CLAN from Milton Keynes were letting nothing impede their progress en route to Murrayfield to watch their Japanese compatriots tackle Scotland in both sides' opening match of the 1991 Rugby World Cup. Thwarted in their efforts to secure an Edinburgh taxi cab, they approached me at the bottom of Fleshmarket Close, thrust £20 into my hands, and promptly requisitioned my vehicle for their services. What else could I do but demur? They were the most charming of kidnappers, regaling me with their admiration for David Sole, Gary Armstrong and Co., expressing their great love of Scotland and the Scottish people, and how, come hell or high water, they were determined to watch their countrymen for as long as they remained in the tournament.

A few hours later, on that Saturday 5 October, the expected outcome – a 47–9 victory for Sole's team – had duly materialised, but it was the unexpected episodes like my sushi-session with the Hamadas which best summed up the second World Cup competition for practitioners of the oval ball game. Unlike the one-sided romp to the winning post enjoyed by David Kirk's All Blacks in 1987, it was the truly global nature of rugby which most lifted one's spirits, the Southern Hemisphere still dominant to be sure, but no longer sweeping all before them.

Dods running (The Scotsman)

Trumpeted beforehand as the biggest sporting event to be staged in Britain since 1966, the Cup was neither the money-spinning catalyst of a world revolution in the sport that some dewy-eyed people were anticipating, nor the over-hyped, over-extended and over-here-gone-tomorrow débâcle the more cynical observers had predicted. Instead, the pursuit of the Webb Ellis Trophy reinforced the view – 'perhaps next time, we'll have four years to work with rather than two' – held by Alan Callan, the former road manager of 1970s super-group, Led Zeppelin, and chairman of CPMA, the Cup's commercial advisers.

However, considering that when the tournament began at a sun-drenched Twickenham on 3 October, less than 12 months had elapsed since the International Board finally and grudgingly accepted that their mission to preserve the amateurism regulations was a self-defeating anachronism, maybe we should just be grateful there was so much that was positive about the competition. The interest generated among people who had never previously demonstrated any enthusiasm for the sport, for instance. And the reams of newsprint and TV footage generated by the most unlikely of sources. The Japanese manager, Shiggy Konno, the former trainee Kamikaze pilot (failed!); the giant Western Samoan piano-shifter, Peter Fatialofa, who charmed the women off the field as much as he terrorised opponents on it; the American, Ray Nelson, who only revealed after the USA's elimination that he had risked paralysis by his participation in the World Cup; and the barrage of love letters dispatched to the Italian camp, whose players made the Chippendales seem like a bunch of weedy adolescents.

Of course, as was nigh inevitable during an event of this magnitude, there were incidents best forgotten. These were exemplified by the cauldron of hate that was the Parc des Princes both before and after England had knocked France out of the competition and Serge Blanco had knocked Nigel Heslop out of consciousness inside the first five minutes, an act which was merely the prelude to a quarter-final tie marred by a whole series of unsavoury flashpoints and which culminated in Gallic coach Daniel Dubroca's assault on the referee, David Bishop. It was difficult to tell which was worse, the actions of the coach, or the snappy, but completely meaningless press conference held the following day in Lille, where the RWC chairman, Russ Thomas, vainly strove to sweep the tunnel incident under the carpet, just one of the occasions when the IB's tunnel vision harked back to the tight-lipped-no-comment-attitude of their officials, which used to be the norm rather than the exception.

One can but hope such a reaction owed more to naivety or misplaced complacency from those concerned than a refusal to come to terms with the perennial problem of violence in rugby, and that the authorities will have established a more credible front three years hence. But whatever blemishes manifested themselves during the World Cup, they should not be allowed to detract from a festival which was in the main, an outstanding success.

And nowhere more so than in Scotland, where the tournament drew television audiences of far greater number than anywhere else in Britain, and which virtually brought the country's capital city to a standstill on five afternoons in October, including a Wednesday lunchtime liaison with Zimbabwe.

Defeat against Romania, a 16–16 draw with the Barbarians and, just days before the main event, an embarrassing defeat at the hands of the Edinburgh Borderers, hardly appeared the ideal preparation for the Scots' anticipated progress to the later stages and a confrontation with the major powers of international rugby, but there was a justified belief in the coaching qualities of Ian McGeechan, even if it was generally recognised that Scottish prospects depended upon their first-choice team staying clear of injuries.

What *was* unarguable was the sense of camaraderie which oozed throughout the squad, the same esprit de corps which had earned them the Grand Slam against the odds in 1990. For the older members of the party, among them John Jeffrey, Finlay Calder, Derek White and Iwan Tukalo, this would be their final bow in the glare of the world's media and, like grizzled old campaigners, there was the tangible feeling that you might beat these men, but you would never break them; while, for the younger players, such as Tony Stanger and Craig Chalmers, the approach of the World Cup made them realise that here was an opportunity to test one's mettle in the same company as the David Campeses and the Grant Foxes of this earth, and also, that four years was a long time to wait for another chance should the script go awry.

Above all, everyone, be it player, pundit, alickadoo or supporter, appreciated that rarely had the omens ever been more in Scotland's favour, given the possibility of home advantage straight through to the final with the psychological impact of turning out at Murrayfield in front of 54,000 paid-up members of the *Flower of Scotland* brigade scarcely to be over-estimated. In retrospect, the fact that the bloom was to wither in the course of a dreadfully disappointing semifinal match with the Auld Enemy, England, served to remind us that an outpouring of nationalist sentiment can have exactly the opposite effect to that intended, placing an

It's not all glamour: squad training (The Scotsman)

excessive burden of expectations on its recipients which stifles rather than inspires ambition. But we had no such thoughts at the beginning of October, only that Scotland were embarking on a new challenge, a new adventure, and that the mood was positively exhilarating.

Sole's men started with that steam-rolling triumph over Japan, who managed to provide a few thrilling passages of play from the possession they received, but badly, from their and the Hamadas' point of view. They were operating on scraps and the longer the game continued, the further Scotland emphasised their superiority, the try count of

What drawers (The Scotsman)

7–1 in their favour a testimony to the way Chalmers sought to move the ball wide at the least opportunity, a feature which regrettably became less visible as the World Cup unfolded.

However, if the game was historic in the sense that when David Milne came on as a replacement for Sole in the 73rd minute, it meant that, together with his more illustrious relations, Iain and Kenny, they had become the first three brothers to be capped for Scotland from the same club (Heriot's) since the Finlays of Edinburgh Academicals in the 1870s, the only traditional aspect of the tussle with the little-fancied Zimbabweans was the confirmation of the paucity of resources at the SRU's disposal and how wonderfully well they have flourished with such lenten fare in the last decade.

The 51–12 scoreline may hardly suggest any serious cause for concern, but the first half saw a decidedly faltering display from what was largely a second-string Scottish team, and though their fitness and mobility saw them overwhelm the Africans in the second period, it was hardly surprising most observers immediately recommended that Sole, Armstrong, the Hastings brothers, Gavin and Scott, and Chalmers should be wrapped in cotton wool for the remainder of the competition.

Nevertheless, at least they were spared the humiliation which had already befallen some of the other leading nations. Fiji and Romania both proved major disappointments, allowing Canada to march into the quarter-finals, albeit as a triumph of industry over entertainment. Still, if anyone wanted amusement, there was always Wales's fall from grace to cheer us up. Prior to the competition, the joke went round the principality that Snow White had returned to her cottage one day to discover it had been burnt to the ground. She started weeping and mourning the loss of her seven little friends, when suddenly she heard a voice from under the rubble. 'Wales for the World Cup, Wales are going to win it ...' 'Oh, thank heavens,' said Snow White, 'at least Dopey's still alive.'

No one was laughing, however, when Wales plummeted to defeat in their opening game against Western Samoa and then slumped out of the World Cup, trounced 38–3 by Australia, their demise made all the worse in the knowledge that they would have to pre-qualify for the 1995 event in South Africa. Yet, whatever the extent of their misery, it was nothing in contrast to the joy of the Samoans, whose uncompromising tackling and All Black-style tactics – many of their players plied their trade in New Zealand – allied to their spontaneous warmth in their numerous public appearances, made them one of the most popular squads in the competition.

Ireland were poles apart from the *manu*-performing islanders, but there was no question which of the two sides gave Scotland the harder contest. Gorging on Caledonian hospitality for a week and being accorded a royal reception wherever they ventured, softened the Samoans up, and, perhaps overly relaxed after reading in the match programme that his opposite number, David Sole, weighed a feeble 5 st 10 lbs (it should, of course, have read 15 st 10 lbs), Fatialofa and his cohorts were taken apart, 28–6, by Scotland, with Jeffrey, White and Calder all producing tremendous performances in the quarter-final encounter.

The Irish had been an entirely different proposition seven days before, in a match characterised by unadulterated courage and unstinting effort from the personnel on both sides, by no stretch of the imagination a classic, but wonderfully compelling to behold. Ireland, bolstered by the kicking of Ralph Keyes, went 15–9 ahead after three quarters of an hour, but the magnificently barnstorming Armstrong first created a try for the debutant Graham Shiel, then touched down himself with just five minutes left, to seal the home side's 24–15 win. Some of the Irish cried foul about Calder's tackle upon their full-back, Jim Staples, claiming that he had altered the whole course of the game by illegal means, but the veteran flanker was exonerated by the referee Fred Howard and the theory discounts the reality that the Scots had, by that stage, assumed control of the line-outs while Irish possession had dried up in the wake of Scottish recovery.

A stirring spectacle, nonetheless, and though Ireland went out of the World Cup in their next game against Nick Farr-Jones's Australia, they came within three minutes of creating the biggest upset of the tournament, Gordon Hamilton's late try, cancelled out by Michael Lynagh's almost desperate dive over the Irish line to bring his team a fraught 19–18 triumph in the most dramatic of circumstances, and leaving us to hope the tournament had truly come alight and that we would be presented with a feast of rugby in the matches ahead.

That it failed to materialise was not merely because the semi-final pairings of Scotland v England at Murrayfield and Australia v New Zealand in Dublin brought together old adversaries, traditional rivals who knew each other's style of play inside out, but also because there was too much that was negative in these fixtures, the fear of losing stifling creativity and rendering the 15-man game an impossible dream.

The build-up to the third meeting between Sole and Will Carling's team within an 18-month period gave us the sight of the Scottish *Sun* printing the words of *Flower of Scotland*, while their southern editions did likewise with, yes, *Swing Low Sweet Chariot*; there was the accusation from one commentator that the English had 'prostituted' the name of rugby by their methods, and the claim in another newspaper that the proceedings would make Bannockburn seem like a kiddies' tea-party. It was blinkered nationalism of the worst kind, and with

England's Brian Moore, an individual always happy to turn a kerfuffle into a full-scale row, upping the already Amazonian temperature with a series of inflammatory comments, it was hardly surprising that the game itself was one of almost stultifying tedium, the ball hardly ever moving beyond the stand-offs, and millions of television viewers left to wonder what all the fuss had been about.

For the record, Rob Andrew's 73rd minute drop goal steered England to a narrow 9–6 victory, though we will never know what might have transpired had Gavin Hastings not fluffed the simplest of penalty attempts, one he would have landed nine times out of ten, with the scores level. All in all, the match represented a sad epitaph for Jeffrey and Calder, both of whom were saying adieu to Murrayfield, after serving their country so marvellously throughout the 1980s.

Twenty-four hours later, Australia booked their passage into the final at Twickenham, but they could not sustain the exciting enterprise which took them to a 13–0 lead in the first quarter, and indeed, appeared satisfied to sit on their advantage, finishing 16–6 winners, and defying everything that the holders, clearly no longer the force of 1987, could hurl at them. Thus it was that a baby girl in Melbourne was bequeathed with the name Harriet Elizabeth Nicola Farr-Jones Davina Campese Wallaby Geddes, but for all the precocious ability of John Eales, Tim Horan and Willie Ofahengaue, and the twinkling menace of Campese and Lynagh, the Australians did not always employ their resources in the best spirit of the game, as they were to prove in the final itself.

Not that they will be complaining, after carrying off the Rugby World Cup in front

Final pressure: Australia v England (World Cup final) (The Scotsman)

of a multinational crowd, which included a sizeable band of Scots giving vent to a whole string of Caledonian battle hymns – and *Waltzing Matilda*! – and endowing the occasion with a festive atmosphere not always apparent on the pitch. Indeed, to their credit, it was the English who, stung by criticism of their supposedly negative attitude, elected to fling the ball around, though the number of instances when passes were spilled illustrated their unfamiliarity with the process in recent

displays. Australia, for their part, thrived on the virtues of hard work, and as in the semi-final, amassed a lead in the opening half, profiting from a Tony Daly try, and then dared England to overhaul them. Despite much perspiration and no little flair, they could not, and a 12–6 margin was sufficient to enable Farr-Jones to climb the stairs to the rostrum and collect the trophy.

It was a merited success over the piece, but whether rugby was also the victor at the

Phew, the garlic! (The Scotsman)

tournament's climax was more open to doubt. Certainly, the game had caught the people's imagination during the World Cup and no one at Murrayfield for the pool games or in Richmond for the final, could fail to be impressed by the scores of youngsters clamouring for Craig Chalmers's autograph, or notice the number of schools, both private and comprehensive, which subsequently took up mini rugby. There was, nevertheless, an excess of sterile play at the expense of the brilliance which sets a competition of this nature apart, and we must ensure that the new law changes help to reduce the number of set pieces which so spoil the flow of any game. Entertainment, above every-thing else, must be the priority.

For the Scots, the World Cup marked the end of one generation and the start of what would probably prove a difficult time of rebuilding. It was said by some that Sole's men did no better than was expected of them, but in their ability to work unceasingly for one another, their willingness to adopt the ploys and stratagems of McGeechan, their sheer hooraymanship, and their refusal to give second best whoever the opposition, the squad were a credit to the SRU and to Scotland. And, if the same can be said of the class of 1995, they will have every reason to feel proud of their achievements.

HOME AFFAIRS

The 1992 Five Nations Championship

Nick Phillip

THERE WAS A real sense of anti-climax about the 1992 Five Nations Championship, following as quickly as it did behind the World Cup. Despite all the records broken by England – they produced their best ever performance at Murrayfield (25–7), highest score against Ireland (38–9), best post-war win over France (31-13), and rounded things off with a 24–0 win over Wales to eclipse the Five Nations record points haul set by the Welshmens' predecessors in 1970 – their second successive Grand Slam possessed none of the drama of their win over France in the decider the previous year or for that matter their loss in even more of an all-or-nothing match in Edinburgh a year earlier.

There was something inevitable about the way in which the side which had established itself in 1991, following a dominant Five Nations performance by finishing runners-up to Australia in the World Cup, eased to a repeat success. The opposition simply did not measure up. Ireland having promised so much the previous year, both in the championship and in the World Cup where they gave the Wallabies their biggest test, flopped terribly to thoroughly deserve the wooden spoon. A humiliating third successive defeat at the Parc des Princes by England

as they completely lost their composure left the French desperately trying to redeem themselves as sportsmen with results becoming a secondary consideration. As for the Welsh, the embarrassment of failing to qualify from the group stages in the World Cup inspired considerable commitment, though it remains evident that they have much to do to translate the quality of their club play to the international arena.

By contrast in recent times it has been a feature of Scottish international performances that the XV selected have drawn on inner resources to produce a level of performance much at odds with the relative mediocrity of the domestic game. This being the case it was perhaps no surprise that having reached the World Cup semi-final the same men could hardly be expected to play above themselves for prolonged spells twice in the same season.

Nonetheless it is a mark of what we in this country have come to expect that such huge disappointment greeted a mere three point defeat at Cardiff Arms Park, a ground at which, as recently as 1982, Scotland had recorded a first win in 20 years. Oddly, though the Scots tasted victory both at home and away and just missed out on claiming

Scotland v Wales (Cardiff) (*The* Scotsman)

Tukalo leads the charge (The Scotsman)

outright second place because of that 15–12 defeat by Wales, the first-half performance in The Royal Bank of Scotland International against England was perhaps the most encouraging Scottish display of the campaign.

'We should have been eight to ten points up at half-time', coach Ian McGeechan said after the side had gone down to a third successive defeat for the first time under his guidance. Instead a touch of inexperience in a team forcibly re-shaped and including four new caps as a consequence of retirements and injuries found itself 10–7 down having expended a massive amount of energy. The craft of Anglo-Scot Neil Edwards on his debut had been a huge factor as Scotland enjoyed some of their best line-out success for years against the Auld Enemy who had expected to be supreme in that phase with 6 ft

10 in Martin Bayfield joining Blackpool Tower Wade Dooley. Policeman Dooley's frustration was perfectly demonstrated with a 'challenge' on Doddie Weir which left the lanky Scot with a worrying ear injury – an incident which amazingly drew no punishment from match officials or those in the England party who saw it replayed several times on television, yet were utterly self-righteous a couple of weeks later when the French lost their discipline in Paris. The best moment of all for the home crowd was the classic double-bluff engineered by David Sole which saw the hugely out-weighed Scots claim a push-over try towards the interval.

Gavin Hastings had an off-day with just one success from five penalty attempts and a couple of Jon Webb penalties allied to a lovely opportunist try for Rory Underwood after an uncharacteristic handling error by the Scottish full-back in midfield provided England with the platform at the break. Gallantly though the Scots defended to restrict their guests to just one more try – a converted Dewi Morris score on the scrum-half's return to the international arena – it was pretty much one-way traffic in the second half with Webb sending over a brace of penalties and the swaggering Jeremy Guscott a spectacular drop-goal.

That said, the Scots managed to stay with their rivals for a full hour as their skipper outlined afterwards. 'We never felt out of the game,' said Sole voicing bewilderment at the way England eased clear. Looking up at the scoreboard midway through the second half and seeing that they were twelve points in front it was hard to work out how they had built up such a lead.

Though inexperience was a factor in conceding the points which took the pressure off England, none of the newcomers let themselves down with Edwards's craft evident in the line-out and flankers David McIvor and Ian Smith – though with a hard job to do in replacing John Jeffrey and Finlay Calder – working away well as a rather more orthodox open and blind-side pair. Scrum-half Andy Nicol, who had to raise his game even more than the rest, having been plucked from Division Two with just a couple of B internationals behind him, and who had been called up to replace the world-class Gary Armstrong when he suffered an appalling knee injury just seven days earlier, arrived as if to the manner born. Little was he to know that within six months he would have toured Hong Kong with the Barbarians Seven, New Zealand with a World XV (during which time he took part in an historic win over the All Blacks), and Australia where he played in two Tests for Scotland. Turning 21 in March, he came of age in a real hurry in rugby terms.

Remarkably though, that was Nicol's 16th international match, having had a long career at schoolboy level and he had yet to taste victory. He was to play a major part in ensuring that he broke his duck a month later in Dublin. The Irish cartoonist who previewed the match by portraying Scottish and Irish line-out jumpers reaching for a wooden spoon was certainly a trifle premature, given that the Scots had reached the World Cup semi-final whilst Ireland had gone so close to beating Australia in one of the best matches of the tournament at Lansdowne Road. Yet big defeats for both countries at the hands of England, allied to the unthinkable Irish home

No way through: Lineen seeks support
(*The* Scotsman)

defeat by the Welsh who had displayed such ineptitude in the World Cup, meant there was an uncharacteristic air of gloom over both supports in the build-up.

The Scottish officials worked hard to ensure that the supporters' doubts did not transmit themselves to the players. Though the dreadful place-kicking of erstwhile World Cup hero Ralph Keyes was an ally to the Scottish cause, a 2–1 try count in an 18–10 win saw Scotland deserved victors on the day. Admittedly, Keyes kicking apart, it might have been a very different story had not the referee adjudged the home side's galloping golden boy Simon Geoghegan offside as he touched down following a delightful grubber kick by the unfortunate Keyes in the first minute, the winger collecting an injury which saw him limp off at the interval. Having declared his imminent retirement at the end of the season, no. 8 Derek White chose the site of his greatest personal triumph, when he scored the two Scottish tries in a narrow win which sparked off Grand Slam success two years earlier, to put on another brilliant display. He provided the scoring pass both for Tony Stanger in the first half, and in a move started and splendidly finished by Nicol as Scotland turned into the wind after the interval. Gavin Hastings converted both tries and put over a penalty in each half as Scotland built up a cushion which left them in a position of some comfort despite the Irish rally which saw Richard Wallace go over for a fine try. Keyes failed to convert and put over just two penalties from a string of straightforward chances. Even the most ardent of Scots was squirming for him as slow handclaps and booing greeted some of his later efforts. His touch also deserted him as he kicked the ball dead from hand on countless occasions to waste Ireland's second-half wind advantage. Cruelly his team manager Ken Reid observed that this was why Keyes hadn't been picked for the previous six years, yet it was only one bad – admittedly downright shocking – game from a player who had done them proud in half-a-dozen previous appearances that season.

The savaging Keyes took from the crowd was nothing to the treatment of the French squad in the media after they lost all semblance of control on the same day as they responded petulantly to a resounding defeat by England. They were to redeem themselves at Parc des Princes against the Irish with a 44–12 win which put some sparkle into a lack-lustre championship, but in between times faced a trip to the ground they hate most. It would be easy to understate the Scottish win because of the combined psychological effects of the French having to overcome both the Murrayfield jinx and prove that they could behave themselves. Yet this match saw Scotland produce a supreme rearguard action. Scotland's defensive qualities had been universally praised throughout the pre-vious couple of seasons, yet they were never better demonstrated than in this encounter. The French pack pummelled them for an hour on a murky day which will have done nothing to dissuade them of the notion that they are simply not meant to win in Edin-burgh. Scotland's first attack produced a try in five minutes, Neil Edwards once again proving himself a master manoeuvrer in the line-out to plunge over from short range and

75 minutes later that score still separated the sides. France encamped themselves in the Scottish half, yet by half-time had only a Jean-Baptiste Lafond penalty to show for their efforts. Early in the second period Lafond's second penalty gave the French the lead for the first time, yet the Scottish response to that score only confirmed any self-doubt the visitors brought into the match as the home pack surged forward to earn the penalty which allowed Hastings to re-establish a one-point advantage. The storm having been weathered, the Scots raised their game in the final quarter and could have won by more than the 10–6 margin opened by a booming Hastings penalty from halfway.

Having made a winning debut coming on for two minutes as a lock against Ireland, Rob Wainwright had better reason to remember his first full game for his country in the more familiar role of flanker. At the other end of the scale, their decisions to retire before the 1992-93 season began having already been made public, 1990 Grand Slam heroes David Sole and Derek White said farewell to the Murrayfield faithful in the best possible way, as winners. Though Sole had declared his intention to tour Australia, White always meant to play his final interna-tional in Wales. After that match he said the occasion had affected his performance, but it would perhaps be a little fanciful to suggest that his popularity explained the jaded nature of the entire team's showing – especially in the first hour.

It would not be over-stating the case to say that Scotland's final championship match was their worst international display for many a season. That they lost just 15–12 and could in fact have won said much more about the quality of the Welsh side than of their visitors. French referee Marc Desclaux twice stopped promising Scottish moves towards the end when match-winning try-scoring opportunites seemed to loom, but the Scots really didn't deserve a victory which would have separated them from the pack as second only to England in the European game. Perhaps most tellingly, the one moment of true inspiration came from a tight-head prop when, his side behind 6–3 with Neil Jenkins early penalty having been overhauled by Gavin Hastings's penalty and Craig Chalmers's drop goal. Huw Williams-Jones produced a turn of pace which left the vaunted Scottish defence in tatters. He released Richard Webster for a try converted by the methodical Jenkins whose place-kicking style did nothing to improve a monotonous affair.

Ahead 9–6 at the break, the agony they had endured over the previous 12 months perhaps made it right that Wales, playing above themselves rather than Scotland, who were well below their best, should take the honours in a match neither side seemed capable of taking by the scruff of the neck. In their defence it should be said that the Scots did once again demonstrate their fighting spirit by raising their game in the final quarter, to be rewarded only by Chalmers's two successful penalty attempts, nullifying two more successes by his opposite number Jenkins. Chalmers took over from Hastings after the full-back missed his fourth of five attempts.

From the outset of the Five Nations campaign when pessimistic Scots supporters

No, that's JJ (The Scotsman)

seemed to have accepted that their side was destined to lose to England, to this disappointing finish in Cardiff, it was a low-key championship. Scotland coach Ian McGeechan would not be drawn to say that the competition had lost some of its importance because of the increasingly global nature of the game, but he did acknowledge that after only the second time of asking, the World Cup was establishing itself as the most important event.

What seemed evident was that players found it very difficult to raise themselves twice in the space of a season, and indeed that was later extended to three times to include the visit to world champions Australia. The reason why this is so much more difficult for the Scots is that, however hard they train, the jump from our domestic rugby is too great. That being the case the SRU are to be

Dominant England (The Scotsman)

Hold on, Doddie. Scotland v Wales (Cardiff) (The Scotsman)

Collectors item – the last Murrayfield ticket before work on the new stands began (The Scotsman)

applauded for proposing and gaining acceptance of an extension to the season by one month. Secretary Bill Hogg has identified this as part of a solution to streamline the national leagues which could also include home and away fixtures, requiring the top players to face each other more frequently, in a more compact set-up. A more glamorous Scottish cup has also become a serious proposition.

The lesson from the English game is that to ensure that players develop the necessary match fitness to operate at international level the domestic game must be structured accordingly. Hence, despite the fact that there are ten times as many rugby players in England as Scotland, half of their international squad comes from a single club – Harlequins.

The difference in league structures may also help to explain one of the bigger controversies of the Scottish international season, namely the number of Anglos in the national side. Complaints were voiced about the inclusion of the likes of Neil Edwards, from the aforementioned Harlequins and Ian Smith, the Gloucester captain, both of whom had previously been involved in English development squads before opting for, in

lock-forward Edwards's case in particular, the rather easier path to international rugby via the Scotland set-up. In both cases, as with several other Scots in the present squad, they took advantage of dual nationality, their accents identifying their links with the Auld country as fairly remote. However the evidence supplied by their efforts during the season completely undermined any notion that their inclusion in any way reduces the Scottish commitment to the cause.

The only legitimate question that might be raised is over the fact that Scotland's selectors are having to look so far afield to find new blood and we return to the massive difference in the standards of club rugby between Scotland and England, France, Wales and for that matter Australia, New Zealand and South Africa. Recognition of that disparity should have us all gasping in disbelief at the way Scotland have managed to perform over the past ten years. Once the infrastructure is overhauled perhaps there will no longer be a case for the SRU to consider appointing an honorary genealogist to look into the family trees of promising players around the globe as has seemed increasingly likely in recent times.

OFF TO SEE THE WIZARDS OF OZ

Scotland's 1992 Tour of Australia

Bill McMurtrie

ONLY THE FUTURE will measure the success of Scotland's 1992 tour to Australia. The playing record was the worst by any Scottish team on a major tour, but the venture will have served its purpose if it produces the players to go as far in the 1995 Rugby World Cup as Scotland went in the 1991 competition.

Only two wins and two draws on the Australian tour could be set against four defeats. Both Tests were lost against the World Cup champions. Yet behind that dismal picture lies a background of adversity.

Not least, Scotland were recasting after the World Cup. Only seven Scots remained for the second Test from the team who lost to New Zealand in the third-place play-off in Cardiff. All four three-quarters were still there, but only Craig Chalmers was left in the middle five and David Sole and Doddie Weir among the tight forwards. Australia had 13 of the team who won the Webb Ellis Trophy by beating England. The gulf in experience was wide even though the Scots had the likes of Sole, Chalmers, Sean Lineen, Scott Hastings, and Iwan Tukalo. How, I wonder, would Australia have fared if, even as world cham-

pions, they had had to dig as deeply into their reserves and to cap five newcomers over the two Tests?

Four of Scotland's new caps were in the pack. Peter Wright and Carl Hogg made their international debuts in the first Test, as did Ian Corcoran, substituting for the injured Kenny Milne, whereas Martin Scott and Kenny Logan joined the capped ranks in the second match of the series.

Moreover, the fixture list was as demanding as any Scotland have faced on tour. Only the 1986 visit to France could match the 1992 tour in the intensity of competition and quality of the opposition, but that does not compare like with like: the 1992 team played twice as many games as their 1986 predecessors, and travelling in France was not the factor that it was in Australia. Between the Scots' first and third venues in Australia they had to travel no less than 4,000 miles, eight hours' flying time. In less than a week they journeyed between Australia's extremes – hot, humid Darwin in the north, and cool, refreshing Hobart in the south of Tasmania.

As in France, home players cropped up

Coach Johnston (The Scotsman)

ber, and others were well past the emerging stage. Not for nothing was David Sole, Scotland's captain, cynical about the overloading. He expressed amazement that Chivas Regal were the tour sponsors. He suggested that Bell's would have been more appropriate when the Australians fielded so many ringers!

Because of the structure of the tour the Scots could not risk too many experiments. A Saturday/Sunday team had to be defined from the start, with few amendments. None of the three young midfield backs – Gregor Townsend, Graham Shiel, and Derek Bain – could be given a run in a weekend match. Scotland had to stand by the tried and tested midfield of Chalmers, Sean Lineen, and Scott Hastings. Nor could Alan Watt be allowed a chance to prove why some of us consider him to be the best front-jumping lock in Scottish rugby. His role was confined to midweek tight-head, though versatility was counted as one of the squad's hallmarks when the 30 players were named in March.

It was significant that no fewer than eight Scots were common denominators in the XVs who played in the weekend games against Queensland and New South Wales and in the two Tests. That number would have been higher but for injuries to Gavin Hastings, Sole, and Kenny Milne.

To lose the opening match against the Northern Territory Invitation XV in Darwin, even though by only one point, was a bad start. A more heartening result followed with a 15-all draw with Queensland at Ballymore, and the Scots then pulled back from a 20-point deficit to draw 24–24 with the Emerging Wallabies in Hobart. The 35–15

more than once against the Scots. Anthony Ekert, the New South Wales reserve scrum-half, appeared in four of the matches, once as replacement, and Garrick Morgan, a young Queensland lock, already a Wallaby, had three games. A handful of others played a couple of games quite apart from those who were in Australia's Test team.

Scotland's opponents in Hobart were Emerging Wallabies in little more than name. Four full-blown caps were among their num-

defeat by New South Wales was the low point of the tour, and it was into the third week before the Scots had their first win, beating New South Wales Country 26–10 in Tamworth.

Yet the Scots did not lose heart. Even after the defeat by New South Wales they believed they could beat Australia, and after the loss of the first Test they still had reason to be hopeful for the second international.

Sole, as captain, deserved great credit for keeping his players together. Nothing exemplified his leadership more than the way he pulled the Scots back in Hobart, when he went on as a replacement, out of position on the open-side flank. Later he switched to his usual role at loose-head, and the Scottish scrummage tightened for the rousing comeback that all but snatched victory.

Sole and his squad had good back-up off the field from Charlie Ritchie as manager, Richie Dixon as coach, and David Johnston as the backs' mentor. Ritchie, though tour manager for the first time, was excellent; quiet but positive, drawing on his wealth of experience as the regular liaison officer for touring teams in Scotland. He knew what his players needed, and he tried to ensure that they had it even though he could do nothing about the dreadful travelling arrangements.

Ritchie was also unstinting in his praise for Dixon and Johnston. The manager was magnanimous in describing them as 'the best coaching partnership in Scotland'. He cited how the pair had worked well together at other levels – with Glasgow and Scotland B as well as on tours to Zimbabwe in 1988 and Japan the following year.

Dixon was already the senior forward coach in the Scottish hierarchy before the tour, but Johnston went to Australia only in the absence of Ian McGeechan and Douglas Morgan. Yet even under duress Johnston instilled the Scottish backs with belief in themselves. The back-play had refreshing, though brief phases of more positive rugby than Scotland had shown since the 1990 tour to New Zealand. It was most obvious in gaining the Scots a 2–1 try count against Queensland. It was apparent also in the first-half of the first Test and the last quarter of both internationals, and the midweek team eventually responded on their last outing, beating Queensland Country 29–12, with four tries to nil.

Sean Lineen, especially, was back on song, regrettably for the last time in Scotland's cause since the Boroughmuir centre confirmed his retirement from international rugby at the end of the tour. The 20-year-old Logan, the first player to be capped out of Stirling County, also responded to Johnston's spell whether as full-back or wing in his seven appearances, two as replacement, and it was a measure of what he had done before that his international debut in the second Test, as Gavin Hastings's stand-in at full back, was his least notable game of the tour. Logan had been chosen to make his debut on the right wing, displacing Tony Stanger, but Gavin Hastings's back strain forced a rethink. Logan was switched to full back, and Stanger kept his place.

Peter Wright deserved much credit for taking over the tight-head vacancy created by Paul Burnell's knee injury in the Cardiff international in March. The Boroughmuir prop had to fit in, and he did so admirably, absorbing the pressure that Queensland turned on him. John Connolly, the Queensland coach, admitted after the drawn match that one facet of his game plan had been to put the screws on the Scots' untested tight head prop.

Wright added another string to his bow when he had to switch to loose-head after Peter Jones's injury in the final midweek match. The Boroughmuir forward adapted well, opening an option for the Scottish selectors to consider to fill the gap left by Sole's retirement.

Carl Hogg displaced David McIvor as Scotland's blind-side flanker, and the Melrose forward also proved himself adaptable to any position in the back row. He played at open side and no. 8, adjusting to suit needs in the matches against the Emerging Wallabies and New South Wales Country, and even though, like any new cap, he admitted to finding the pace of the first Test well beyond his expectation, he was worthy of his place in the Melrose list of international forwards, among them his uncle, Jim Telfer.

Ian Corcoran was pitched into international rugby only eight minutes into the first Test when Milne tore calf muscles, but it was not a happy debut for the Gala hooker. The Scottish scrummage, secure with Milne, creaked too often and once rolled over backwards under a hefty shunt from the Australian pack, though Corcoran had the consolation of taking a strike against the head.

Milne's tour replacement, Martin Scott, had one obvious edge over Corcoran. He was bulkier than the Gala hooker, more in Milne's build, and when he proved his fitness

in the game against Queensland Country he set himself up for his Test debut, the first cap out of Dunfermline since Ron Glasgow in 1965.

Logan, Wright, Hogg, and Scott had a common denominator. Each could talk positively about the game and his role in rugby. Logan summed up his exuberant confidence by describing how he could convince himself that he could do anything that he tried to do, whether it be only catching a high ball, Wright chatted easily about his 'bad boy' days and his reformed attitude to rugby, Hogg was enthusiastic about how eager he was to make up for time lost through injury, and Scott, though surprised to be on the tour, had no inhibitions before his Test debut. Outwardly, he was so relaxed that he might have been playing for Dunfermline against, say, Kirkcaldy.

Scott's cap, however, did raise a question about the tour selection. Not why was he chosen for the Test ahead of Corcoran, the nominated second hooker for the tour, but why was Scott not there in the first place? After all, Scott had played in the B internationals against Ireland and France in the past season, with Corcoran as back-up each time, and the Dunfermline hooker had not let Scotland down, even though both matches were lost. Yet when the tour squad was named in March the selectors listed Corcoran as reserve to back up Milne and John Allan. Scott came into the frame only as stand-by when Corcoran was promoted to the tour squad after Allan had withdrawn. No answer was forthcoming as a solution to that conundrum. Those who knew were not saying.

Not only did new caps emerge with

credit. Johnston cited Graham Shiel as mature beyond his years in holding the midweek team's midfield backs together, and Damian Cronin deservedly came back to international rugby in the second Test, his twenty-third cap. The London Scot stood beside Sole and Milne in commendations for consistency, a sharp contrast to the Cronin who had been an inconsistent tourist in Zimbabwe, Japan, and New Zealand.

Cronin pointed to Dixon's man-management skills as a reason why he flourished on tour. Quite simply, the coach helped to give Cronin the urge to play for a place back in the international team. The London Scottish forward, deposed by Doddie Weir for the World Cup, emerged as the Scots' outstanding midweek forward, and his perseverance paid off when he was recalled to displace Neil Edwards as left lock for the second Test. I would have had Cronin in for the first Test.

Cronin's line-out work was a plus mark in the opening game. Generally the team were inconsistent even though John Robertson and Stuart Reid scored good support tries, and Darwin's evening temperature, a fierce afterglow of 30-plus in mid-afternoon, was not all that was too hot for the Scots. Five guests boosted Northern Territory to a headlong charge, and not even a 13–7 lead early in the second half, after Reid's try, was enough to generate impetus within the Scottish ranks. Townsend's drop goal seemed to have saved the Scots, but Ekert replied with a penalty goal for a 17–16 win.

Three days later, with more amenable conditions in Brisbane, the Scots had a highly satisfactory result with the draw with Queensland. It was better than either of Scotland's two previous touring teams had had against the same state. It was also more than England, Wales, and France had managed in the two previous years.

Courage and application in defence were the hallmarks of the Scots' performance, especially when they faced a stiff breeze in the second half. They had to work with limited possession, all the more difficult when more than half of the team were rusty after seven or eight weeks out of match-fitness, and although Queensland exerted enormous pressure for much of the game the tourists did not wilt. It was the fire that steeled Wright and Hogg for their Test debuts two weeks later.

Scotland had to recover from the loss of a soft try to Tim Horan after only five minutes' play. Their response was to take a 12–6 lead within eight minutes. Milne's long throw-in to Lineen set up the first try, Derek Stark snapping it up when Paul Carozza failed to clear from Chalmers's chip to the right, and a fierce phase of three successive rucks led the way for Andy Nicol, Gavin Hastings, Stark, and Scott Hastings to lay on a try for Lineen. Gavin Hastings converted both from well out on the right. Not even the loss of Gavin Hastings early in the second half upset the Scots' resolve. Logan took over at full-back as if to the manner born.

On down to Hobart, with its cool airs and a picturesque setting at Bellerive Oval. The Scots, however, were rocking when the so-called Emerging Wallabies led 24–4 after 50 minutes when David Knox stretched his 100 per cent kicking record with his sixth goal. The tourists' one score was a try that

Hogg plundered from loose line-out ball, and it was only after the Emerging Wallabies had lost Matt Ryan that Sole stirred the tourists to recovery. Ryan was sent off for punching Watt, who had to be taken off with a painful jaw.

Thereafter, with Sole in the van, the Scots swept back with tries by Cronin, Shiel, Stark, and Milne inside quarter of an hour. Peter Dods could convert only two, and the Scots, letting slip two other chances of tries, had to settle for a draw.

Scotland went into the New South Wales match without their two most senior players, the captain and vice-captain. Sole had taken a knock on a knee in the Hobart match, and Gavin Hastings had not recovered from his leg injury at Ballymore. Ian Smith took over as captain, but the Scots struggled to hang on to a match that New South Wales eventually won by 35–15.

Instead of improving, the Scots seemed to be slipping. The humbling result at Waratah Rugby Park, formerly Concord Oval, was a disappointment after the encouraging draw with Queensland. Even Scotland's defence, resilient and aware in Brisbane, was too readily broken as New South Wales ran in six tries, with just five goals in response by Craig Chalmers.

Scotland, only seven points down, were still in the game early in the second half when Willie Ofahengaue, though blatantly offside at a maul, intercepted a Lineen pass and ran from halfway to score. It was the killer blow, and though Chalmers cut back again with his fourth penalty goal New South Wales completed the rout with tries by Marty Roebuck and Peter Jorgensen in the last seven minutes.

After the match we experienced the freedom and razzamatazz that Australian rugby needs to market itself to compete with other codes. The press, the five Scots included, had unhindered access to the New South Wales dressing-room for interviews. Nick Farr-Jones, Australia's World Cup captain, gave us five minutes of his time while BBC radio was told to wait its turn, and outside in the concourse a jazz band played merrily away to entertain the supporters waiting to mingle with the players and to hear the after-match speeches. Such antipodean functions are usually held in camera, with a few invited guests to augment the match personnel. Not in Sydney. Imagine it happening at Murrayfield!

Upcountry at Tamworth three days after the Sydney match, the Scots at last found a win, beating New South Wales Country 26–10 on the Rugby League ground at Scully Park, though it was not an easy gain. The vital surge came in the three minutes before the interval when Townsend dropped a goal, the agonisingly inconsistent David Millard forced his way over from a five-metre scrum, and Dods converted. Individually Hogg, Cronin, and Logan played themselves to the verge of the Test team. Only Hogg, however, was called on from that trio. Cronin and Logan had to wait for the second Test.

Scotland could look back with relief on the Tamworth match. The sentiment, though, was completely different four days later in the Test at the Sydney football stadium. The Scots were exasperated that they had let slip a game they could have won. Twenty minutes of slack, uncontrolled rugby after the interval cost them dearly. It

Young stars: Craig Chalmers and Graham Shiel (The Scotsman)

was a phase out of character with the Scots' game for the other hour of the match.

Scotland wrested a 9–7 half-time lead by dint of steady rugby in the face of severe pressure up front. The Scottish scrummage rocked after Milne's injury departure, and they gained too little in the line-out. John Eales won his duel with Doddie Weir, and the majority of Scotland's touchline successes came off Rob Wainwright at the tail. One produced the Scots' try. Wainwright not only creamed ball for Wright to peel, but the no. 8 was up in support to score on the other flank after Chalmers's up-and-under and Lineen's follow-up. Gavin Hastings converted from well out on the right.

Scotland could have won if they had turned the screws after the interval. Instead, they relaxed. Concentration was lost, especially by Gavin Hastings, and Australia snapped up 10 points in 12 minutes. Carozza exploited Michael Lynagh's hack ahead for a try, and Lynagh kicked two of his four goals. Carozza went on to score his second try, as did David Campese. It was the third time Campese had scored two tries in an international against Scotland.

In the midweek game between the two internationals Peter Dods took his leave of rugby by leading the Scots to a 29–12 win over Queensland Country at Toowoomba. It was his last game after 11 tours with Scotland and one with the Lions.

Other retiring tourists, Sole and Lineen, did not have such a happy departure, even though each scored a try in the second Test at Ballymore. The Scots conceded too many penalties for them to secure a first-half platform. The penalty count at the interval was 13–7 and the scoreboard read 16–3, and though the Wallabies stretched to 27–3 after 51 minutes the Scots did not give up. They matched Australia in tries and points in the final quarter.

Afterwards Sole was severely critical of the Test refereeing by Colin Hawke, and he was fully justified. The New Zealander was inconsistent at the line-out and in refereeing the ball on the ground. The Scots suffered, though they had learned to live with poor refereeing throughout the tour. Not one of the Australians who refereed the six non-international matches was in the same league as the late Kerry FitzGerald.

Yet, like the other disadvantages the Scots faced, the refereeing did not sour the tour. It was accepted as part and parcel of touring and – for the younger players – growing up.

LETTER FROM DOWN UNDER

A Report on Rugby in Australia and New Zealand

Richie Dixon

UPON LEAVING my first club, Duns in Berwickshire, and enrolling at Jordanhill College of Education in 1966, I was soon made aware of the influence New Zealand rugby had on that of Scotland.

Bill Dickinson, the Jordanhill College coach – later to become the first coach of Scotland – soon converted me from full-back to the role of inside-centre as performed by the then All Black second five-eighth, Keith McRae. This of course was to bring the forwards back into play away from the set piece. Bill constructed packs for Jordanhill College, Glasgow and Scotland along the New Zealand lines; i.e. with forwards who were powerful, aggressive, mean, mobile, and totally uncompromising. Bill loved it and I still have the marks to prove it.

Since then Jim Telfer, Derrick Grant and Ian McGeechan have further reinforced this New Zealand influence upon our game. Make no mistake, first, last and always, all four men are Scots, but having been coached by or having coached with all of them, I can appreciate very much how they have moulded various aspects of the New Zealand game into Scottish rugby. Jim Telfer in particular set Scotland on the way to a rucking game based on the New Zealand model during the early '80s and to my mind it was he who encouraged a generation of coaches to follow and develop his lead. Scotland can only be grateful for such a man. While we have adapted parts of the New Zealand game to suit our purposes, what of New Zealand rugby itself, its structure and approach to the game?

The New Zealand Rugby Football Union (NZRFU) has under its control 27 provinces, split into three sets of nine (North, Central, South), about 600 clubs and an estimated 200,000 men and boys playing the game each season. As in all countries the clubs form the bed-rock of the game but in my opinion it is the provinces that produce the force of New Zealand rugby. A top provincial player may play a mere handful of games for his club side, and in a particularly busy representative season perhaps none at all. In either case he will play far fewer games than an equivalent player in Scotland. Apart from inter-provincial matches, the top four provinces along with two Australian state sides take part in a tournament known as the

Super Six. Let there be no doubt as to the quality of such a tournament – some believe it to be of better quality than the Five Nations Championship in the Northern hemisphere. As from next season, should the right conditions prevail, the Super Six will become the Super Ten with the addition of four top South African provinces. With that standard of competition between a minimum of 150 of the best players in the Southern hemisphere it should be easy to understand how much more difficult it will be for us in Scotland to maintain our position in world terms.

In New Zealand, clubs and provincial coaches follow a national policy in terms of a framework for coaching. National and provincial coaching courses are based on materials provided by the NZRFU coaching sub-committee and the National Director of Coaching, Mr Lee D. Smith. There are three levels of coaching accreditation. These are progressive courses, each having a menu of basic themes. Course one: the character of the game, individual skills, unit skills and team skills. Course two: technical or skill development, psychological development (motivation) and tactical development. The role of the coach, teaching skills and skill analysis are also covered in this course. Course three: theoretical topics, organisational topics and practical topics. The manuals containing the materials for each course are not presented as definitive books on coaching but rather as a sound base for coaching and as reference resources. These courses are usually run pre- and early season and will be of five or six days' duration.

In addition to the National Director of

Awaiting the forwards: Richie Dixon
(The Scotsman)

Coaching, thirteen of the provincial unions have a salaried director of coaching. The bigger provincial unions may well have more than one salaried coach. These salaried staff perform the role of development officers similar to these employed by the Scottish Rugby Union, the only real difference being that New Zealand have directors of coaching and many more development officers. The NZRFU has complete control over the employment of development officers within the provincial unions. As the provincial unions utilise national materials, it is easy to see how a national policy or philosophy can be implemented and sustained. I would add

Leading the world. Australia v New Zealand (The Scotsman)

that there is room for individual interpretation within the basic framework thereby allowing individual coaches to marshal their resources within the limitations or strengths of their own players and teams.

The approach to rugby in New Zealand is much more intensive and competitive than the approach to the game in Scotland. To become a top-class provincial player and ultimately an All Black is to achieve a status known to only a very few players in this country. Rugby is the national game of New Zealand and having celebrated their centenary with a three test series against a World XV – coached by Ian McGeechan and including David Sole, Gavin Hastings, Derek White and Andy Nicol – they will be trying to build upon what must be one of the best records for any sport in terms of consistent success at the top level. Because rugby is their national game, the most obvious asset they have is the number of men and boys playing each season. This coupled with the status achieved by players can encourage people to stay in the game after leaving the playing field for the last time. Provincial competition and coaching are two of the factors involved in producing more players capable of contending for international selection. In other words, through sheer weight of numbers, good intense competition and coaching, New Zealand are likely to have many more players trying to achieve international status than we will ever have.

New Zealand have the structure and approach which enables them to maintain their position in world rugby. They are not, however, complacent in this knowledge: New Zealand will explore every avenue available to them with the object of continually improving both in terms of domestic and international rugby football.

Australia since the early '80s has also had an effect on our rugby, with particular reference to back play. This has not been so easily recognised in terms of our domestic league rugby but it has certainly come into the thinking at national level.

Do not be fooled into believing that Australia play running rugby at all times, this may be the overall impression, often reflected in their points total in any given game. In real terms they apply a tactical astuteness from a strong forward set-piece base and in the main are capable of playing tight, up the middle and wide. By mixing up these three methods of playing the game, i.e. making the right decisions based upon quality of possession, they have become very adept at turning pressure into points. Australian players can be particularly innovative and because of their high skill levels can keep the target moving in order to exploit an opponent's defensive weakness. This is particularly noticeable when they are attacking a splintered defence in broken play.

Why, in the last 12 years or so, have Australia developed into a consistent major force in world rugby? Perhaps part of the answer is pressure from within Australia itself. Whereas New Zealand have the constant pressures of maintaining the status of their national game and sustaining their proud record of achievement, Australian rugby has to cope with rather different pressures. To most of the Australian population, the focus of team games is very much on either Australian rules or Rugby League.

These two codes are very much the top two, attracting players, sponsorship, television coverage and newspaper column inches. The Australian Rugby Football Union (ARFU) therefore has to preside over a game which has to work hard to attract firstly, young players into the game, and secondly, spectators. The ARFU believe they have to present a game – at all levels – which is attractive to both. There is innovative but nonetheless forceful marketing of the game. In other words, they feel they have to compete on the same terms as the top two codes. This provides a very strong incentive to produce good, attractive rugby football.

In terms of coaching, I believe Australian coaches follow the New Zealand model of progressive coaching courses. The top coaches may well study methods used in Australian rules and Rugby League – it would be difficult not to, considering the exposure these two codes receive. One major difference and advantage in terms of player development is the Australian Institute of Sport (AIS) – funded by the Government and based in Canberra. The AIS has centres in each of the states and these centres are to the best of my knowledge funded by the Federal State Government. The ARFU can use the AIS to develop and monitor individual development programmes for selected players. These players can be identified whilst still playing schools or age-group rugby but not exclusively so. The main advantage of the AIS is the bringing together of expertise from many disciplines. For example, experts in physical conditioning, psychological development and dietary awareness. This pool of knowledge ensures that all factors involved in producing suitable programmes can be collated and selected appropriately to suit each individual's requirements. Whilst on these programmes, suitable skills coaching and playing-performance monitoring will also take place. Having identified potential talent, this can be developed within a given timescale in order to progress to performance at the highest level, in this case the Australian Test team. The added advantage of course is that any player attending AIS programmes will be exposed to a cross-section of sporting performers all striving for excellence within their own discipline. Success does breed success.

The ARFU then has responded to the pressures from within, harnessed its resources and moved, as it would see it, with the times in forms of sponsorship and promotion of the game. Indeed the profile of Rugby Union is probably higher than at any other time in the history of the ARFU. Obviously winning the William Webb Ellis Trophy (RWC) was a tremendous achievement and with Queensland becoming the first Australian winners of the Super Six tournament, rugby in Australia is likely to go from strength to strength during the '90s.

These notes on rugby in New Zealand and Australia are not intended to be all-embracing but hopefully will have given some idea of the background to the obvious rugby strengths each country has.

No escape: Doddie gets his man (The Scotsman)

Iwan Tukalo eyes a chance (The Scotsman)

THE SEASON
AHEAD

OVERVIEW

An Assessment of Scotland's International Hopes

Norman Mair

THE BRITISH BOXER who said of an impending fight in America that he would have to win on a knock-out to get a draw would have struck a chord with many a rugby side touring in foreign climes. But the Scotland players, who had been on the receiving end in both last summer's Tests against the Wallabies in the Australians' own backyard, knew that the gap between them and the World Champions was not to be explained away by the difficulties they had had with refereeing interpretations.

Nor would it have been wise to make too much of the fact that England had been roundly trounced in Australia before returning home to reach the World Cup final and capture a second successive Grand Slam. The sheer physical scale of the English forwards, and the blazing pace within their three-quarter line, always suggested that Australia would again find the Poms a different proposition once they were back in their native hemisphere.

All that said, there will be nothing defeatist about the note sounded by the Scotland coach, Ian McGeechan, and his henchmen, Douglas Morgan and Richie Dixon, as the build-up begins for the 1993 Five Nations Championship. 'There is,' McGeechan maintains, confidently enough, 'sufficient material to ensure that if we play as we can, we can give even France at Parc des Princes and England at Twickenham a run for their money or more' – his choice of idiom being perhaps accidental!

McGeechan consistently refused to accept publicly that the 1992 Championship, in the wake of the World Cup, was a season

Gregor Townsend in typical mode
(*The* Scotsman)

of transition because that very phrase in itself offers an excuse for losing. Yet one does not doubt that privately that was how he saw it.

Similarly, where the trip Down Under to take on a Wallabies XV still trailing clouds of glory was concerned, there can have been few who were not a deal more optimistic as to the long-term benefits than they were about the Test match scorelines awaiting the tourists.

However, there is one worry which none among Scotland's coaching hierarchy has attempted to minimise. Namely, how to fill the void left by the sadly early retirement of David Sole. 'As captain,' says McGeechan, 'David went about his business quietly. He was no tub-thumper but he carried so much respect among his fellow players that he had no need to be.

'In his own way, he was, as Nick Farr-

Jones so warmly acknowledged after first-hand experience of him with the World XV which beat the All Blacks, a very good motivator, not least through the example he himself invariably set from kick-off to no-side. As captain of Scotland, he understood perfectly the game we wanted to play – indeed, needed to play – and he was excellent at isolating what really mattered and hammering it home.

'He took responsibility readily and you would see him taking the forwards into the bar for a drink and know that the time was being put to telling use. On the field, too, he showed himself a good tactician – as, for instance, in the way he protected a lead against the wind in the closing quarter of last season's Ireland match at Lansdowne Road, keeping it tight, using the narrow side, playing to retain the put-in at the next scrum. Not spectacular but the right tactics at the right time.'

Not least because he had served in his own Scotland days under Ian Mclauchlan, whom he rated an outstanding captain, McGeechan was assuredly in no way averse to having his side led from loose head.

Though he had his critics as a scrummager, Sole was, as McGeechan is always quick to emphasise, 'never found wanting when the rest of the tight five were of the requisite calibre – as they were, for instance, with the Lions'.

It is, though, in other aspects of forward play that Sole is likely to be most sorely missed. Still the fastest of the Scotland pack as recently as the 1991 World Cup, he was the proverbial host in himself in the realms of sweeping and tackling, driving and rucking.

A playmaker whom the manager, Clive Rowlands, picked out on the eve of the 1989 series with the Wallabies as quite possibly the Lions' key player – 'and what Welshman ever thought he would live to say that not of a stand-off or other back but of, may God forgive us, a prop forward!'

No less an authority than Iain Milne has opined that Alan Watt could conceivably have a future as the Scotland loose head but, aside from the fact that Watt's heart has not always seemed to be in making it as an international prop, the front runner at the close of Scotland's antipodean venture was still held to be Peter Jones.

In contrast to the erstwhile lock that is the gargantuan Watt, the Gloucester man is on the small side. Of course, if Paul Burnell were to reclaim his tight-head berth, it is not impossible that Peter Wright, who excited favourable comment in the course of figuring in both of the Australian Tests, could be tried out in his less familiar role as a loose head.

The plight of the Scotland scrum in the Land of Oz confirmed the suspicion that, with the possible exception of the All Blacks at the Arms Park, the only really good scrum which Scotland met last season was England's and even at that only in the World Cup, not in the Calcutta.

Kenny Milne, in the 1992 Five Nations Championship, demonstrated afresh that he has the scrummaging presence which almost any permutation of Scotland's current forward resources is patently going to require. What is more, his much more assured throwing in had not little to do with the emergence of Neil Edwards as, to the eye of McGeechan, 'the best front jumper in the

Five Nations Championship'.

Edwards, though, lost much ground in Australia. The fact that he was dropped for the second Test means that the Scotland lock-forward coupling is wide open, events in Australia surely strengthening the case for playing the talented and telescopic, highly mobile Doddie Weir either at no. 8 or on the blind side.

Significantly, the former Melrose and Scotland three-quarter, Keith Robertson, who had played so much club rugby with him, believes that, within a couple of seasons, the lanky, ball-playing Weir could be doing for Scotland many of the things in the broken play which Finlay Calder used to do so profitably.

There was hardly a viewer back home among Scottish rugby's cognoscenti who did not make the same comment with regard to Scotland's Test match loose-forward trio – to wit, that while Messrs Smith, Wainwright and Hogg all, to differing degrees, did well, they were never remotely the kind of integrated back-row unit which Scotland had come to take for granted in the days of Finlay Calder, Derek White and John Jeffrey. Moreover, those three musketeers were the stuff which tries are made of: sundry Scottish scores had their origin in some dextrous, split-second opportunism by Calder while Jeffrey and White jointly share the try-scoring record for a Scotland forward with 11 apiece.

Now playing with much more of the belligerence befitting a former Cambridge University boxing Blue, the naturally athletic Rob Wainwright, in addition to a useful turn of foot, is a gifted line-out jumper. Were

Stay big David (The Scotsman)

Joy. Almost a smile from Jim Telfer
(The Scotsman)

Scotland to pick both Wainwright and Weir for their back row, they would not only have a strong hand toward the tail of the line-out to help offset any limitations elsewhere but they would be well on the way to outnumbering the enemy jumpers in, say, a four or five man line-out.

The new laws, which will be in force next season, could affect selection. These are very early days but McGeechan reckons that even if the game is faster, teams will still want plenty of size to knock men back in the tackle, making it harder for the opposition to dictate the ensuing maul or ruck and thereby engender the quick and fluent possession which the law changes would seem to necessitate.

Behind the scrum, there are three fascinating facets to the early season debate with pride of place going to the rivalry at scrum-half between Gary Armstrong and the 21-year-old Andy Nicol. Britain's Young Player of the Year, Nicol followed up the rich promise of his baptismal season in the Five Nations Championship, in which he showed from the very first the wisdom of backing class, by playing superbly for the World XV versus the All Blacks. Predictably, he had a much more difficult passage against the Wallabies, partly because forewarned is forearmed and Farr-Jones and company had seen him at close quarters in New Zealand, but mainly because he was behind badly beaten forwards. Gifted though he is, the quick-footed Nicol will surely have to go some to hold off the more powerfully built, battle-hardened Armstrong, with his ability to put even bad ball to good use and to get in among the game of even the best of enemy scrum-halfs. One way and another, an argument which could split the country, not least geographically.

At long last, there is again some pace about with Derek Stark and the exciting Kenny Logan, the latter of whom made his international debut at full-back versus the Wallabies, waiting in – and on – the wings. Nonetheless, initially at any rate, still more interest will attach to the identity of Sean Lineen's successor at second five-eighth cum inside-centre, Scotland's Kiwi having decided to retire from the international arena.

'Sean,' declared McGeechan, by way of a parting salute, 'has been invaluable, particularly in the infectious way he has brought something of the New Zealand approach to the furnace that is the midfield confrontation. The aggression in both attack and defence, the particular skills involved, the lines to run, the angles to exploit ... Above all perhaps, the importance of giving the back row something to work off and vice versa.'

As the whistle sounds on the new season, Lineen's jersey would seem to lie between Graham Shiel and the uncapped teenager, Gregor Townsend: between, in the graphic but valid oversimplification, a player with the swift and suave hands to make the ball beat the man, and one with the break to do it himself. Townsend – who, as most of Scottish rugby is so well aware, grew up as a stand-off and played there on the Australian tour – prefers outside-centre to inside. Again, it is known that McGeechan has long fancied him more in the former role. Nonetheless, the thinking is that Scott Hastings, for all his diverse attributes, has not got the command of pass which an inside-centre has to have. Consequently, if Townsend, whose game is shot through with moments of real brilliance, is to figure in the Scotland XV as a centre, it would maybe have to be as a second five-eighth.

Either Shiel, who stayed on in Australia to further his rugby education, or Townsend would represent a change of style. Lineen, unusually for a New Zealand second five-eighth, is no great kicker whereas both of the young Borderers would be capable of utilising the angles of punt available one pass out from first five-eighth or stand-off. Which could be important if the first impression of Farr-Jones, after the opening Test in the Bledisloe Cup, were to prove correct and kicking play an even greater part under the new laws than under those which immediately preceded them.

It can be a long, long time not just, as the song has it, from May to December but from September to January. Much could happen in respect of changing personnel between now and The Royal Bank of Scotland International with Ireland at Murrayfield on January 16, 1993. In truth, last winter, by the time Scotland played their first match in the Five Nations Championship, against England at Murrayfield, Ian Smith, David McIvor and Neil Edwards, none of whom had even managed to make the previous summer's understrength tour to North America, had all played themselves into the Scotland pack.

With that reservation, McGeechan expects that Scotland will still be seeking, as in recent seasons, to make up for a certain lack of size and bulk up front and individual speed behind the scrum, by getting the ball out wide and setting a hurrying tempo, and by playing out of the tackle with a degree of continuity which they clearly found beyond

That's my boys (The Scotsman)

Swift away (The Scotsman*)*

them against the World Champions.

England, with some of the performances of their B team in New Zealand underlining their advantages in the matter of numerical resources and therefore depth, will once more start the championship as weighty favourites. But even they will know the difference when Wade Dooley does actually follow Paul Ackford into retirement. They could also miss the prolific finishing of Rory Underwood although they would appear to

have the ultimate in ready made replacements in the person of his younger brother, Tony.

The hope is that, by the time Scotland go to Twickenham in March, they will have a Triple Crown in their sights, although McGeechan is sensibly wary not just of Wales, who beat Scotland at the last time of asking, but also of Ireland.

In spite of manifold disasters, points out McGeechan, the Irish have, within the last year, given first the Wallabies and then the

All Blacks one hell of a fright. Nor should anyone overlook the fact that several of their core players, the men around whom their side would normally be constructed, were not on their New Zealand tour.

As for Wales, it is impossible for a Scot, shrugs McGeechan, not to envy them their club rugby while, under Robert Norster, as team manager, and Alan Davies, as coach, they are plainly getting their overall structure right. Besides which, players such as Emyr Lewis at flank forward and Scott Gibbs in the centre have it in them to lift a side.

Scotland, alas, have not won in Paris since Jim Telfer scored the winning try at Colombes Stadium in 1969 but McGeechan talks less of that Parc des Princes hoodoo than of the effect he is convinced Pierre Berbizier will have on the Tricolors: 'As their coach, he knows what is needed and is not too proud to say that he thinks that there are areas where France can learn from Scotland. But he knows also that they must be true to their own heritage.'

It is not just because Scotland have to travel to Parc des Princes and Twickenham that so many will read a lot more into Scotland's chances in 1994 than 1993: it is also because there is a Lions' tour to New Zealand in the summer of '93. All three of Scotland's Grand Slams – 1925, 1984 and 1990 – have followed hard upon Lions' tours. To South Africa in 1924, to New Zealand in 1983 and to Australia in 1989. On each of those missions, there was a sizeable Scottish contingent who returned home having assimilated much from friend and foe alike and, probably still more pertinently, having shed any inferiority complex they may previously have had with regard to the more glamorous players of the other Home Unions.

LOOKING AHEAD

The League Season in Prospect

Graham Law

SCOTLAND'S NATIONAL LEAGUES, an innovation in their day, are perhaps about to enter a watershed season, their 20th, in 1992–93. The decision to follow suit and embrace a league structure in England, Wales and Ireland – where, for the most part, the frequency of testing fixtures is greater in the upper echelons – leads some observers to conclude that 14-club divisions do not stimulate the intensity required to prepare our players for the rigours of the international game.

At the other end of the scale, clubs who have to rely on bar turnover, membership fees and occasional support from self-generated sponsors, can face daunting travel schedules. Last season, for example, Division Seven champions, Berwick, had to journey to RAF Kinloss, the sort of trip which can eat into hard-earned club monies, especially given the need to foster youth interest in the game. That is why the backing, initially of Schweppes and now of McEwan's, for the national leagues, has been vital for the well-being of the clubs.

How should the leagues develop? I would like to see four divisions of eight clubs, playing home and away, operating at national level, with district divisions running below that tier, from which the champion clubs could still win promotion. Such a set-up would partially counter the argument, with which I have much sympathy, that to tinker with the national leagues would close the door on any attempt to follow Highland, Preston Lodge, Stirling County and Currie and march up the divisions. Whatever happens, the Scottish Rugby Union is sure to monitor events as it has demonstrated its desire in recent years to countenance change when it is for the good of the game.

The key question in this season's First Division campaign revolves around whether Melrose can lift the title for the third time in four seasons. Director of coaching, former Scottish international and British Lion, Jim Telfer, will be at the helm again, cajoling, hectoring, but, above all, encouraging his players to find higher levels. Telfer is likely to be able to call upon most of the players who secured Melrose's championship last season; their only setbacks occurred when they drew with Edinburgh Academicals and were defeated in a howling gale at Meggetland by Boroughmuir.

Five of the Melrose side, centres Graham Shiel and Derek Bain, stand-off Craig Chalmers, lock Doddie Weir, and

Tense stuff.
Melrose v Edinburgh Accies
(*The* Scotsman)

Best mates. Sean and Scott but Boroughmuir won (The Scotsman)

no. 8/flanker Carl Hogg, were members of Scotland's summer tour party to Australia, while Hogg joined full back Craig Redpath and hooker Steve Brotherstone as members of the Scottish side who competed in the Students World Cup in Italy in July. Shiel and Bain stayed on in Australia at the end of the Scottish tour, enhancing their rugby education by playing for clubs in the Sydney area. The accumulation of the lessons learned on these overseas stints will stand Melrose in good stead, as will their continued attention to development of their own talent.

Led by a team of coaches including the likes of Les Allan and Norman Elliot, the Greenyards is a vibrant place as various age-group sides are put through their paces. Melrose, who will be captained for a second

Watsonians launch the brothers Hastings and Johnston (The Scotsman)

season by that tireless second-row, Robbie Brown, extended the repertoire of their back moves last season, when their former three-quarter, Rob Moffat, was enlisted to assist with the coaching. Moffat, a PE teacher in Galashiels, has relinquished the reins of Scottish schools coach, a post he held for seven years, to concentrate on club duties this season. When such talents as Andy Purves, Gary Parker, Ross Brown, Bryan Redpath, Andrew Kerr and Andrew Redpath are thrown into the equation, it is clear Melrose will be hard to restrain. That said, it will be intriguing to see how they cope with the injury absence of Keith Sudlow at tight head prop, a loss which might well be exacerbated if Tom McLeish on the loose-head cannot be persuaded to continue.

Down boy. Edinburgh Accies v Heriot's (The Scotsman)

Melrose, assuming key personnel remain fit, might be most pundits' tip for honours. Where should one look for the strongest challenge?

Probably to the capital, whose five First Division clubs finished within the top eight places last season. Edinburgh Academicals were runners-up last season and though they will be without their international front-row duo, Scotland captain David Sole (who retired after the Australian tour), and hooker John Allan (who returned to South Africa to be married), they will again field a formidable pack, buttressed by the reappearance of Jeremy Richardson. The lock, an erstwhile captain of Scotland B, represented Glasgow High-Kelvinside last season, but a change of job will see him back on his old stamping

Even the President can join in: Jim Russell of Melrose (The Scotsman)

ground. One significant new face will be Martin Scott, the 26-year-old North and Midlands hooker and product of Dunfermline. Scott was called out to Australia during the summer as a replacement for Kenny Milne, injured in the first Test, and made such an impact that he was duly granted his debut in the second. Maintaining the interest from north of the Forth are the international back-row forwards David McIvor and Rob Wainwright, having indicated his willingness to travel from his army posting in Catterick. Look out, too, for Malcolm McVie, a beanpole second-row who won national under-21 honours while studying at St Andrews University last season and who spent the summer playing in South Africa. In the backs, scrum-half Derek Patterson has been sharpened by a trip to Durban. Outside him, the main problem for Academicals' coaches Hugh Campbell and Bob Easson will be accommodating a welter of pace and guile, epitomised by Alex Moore and Rowen Shepherd.

Heriot's are one of three teams who have retained their place among the First Division élite since the leagues were introduced in 1973–74. (Hawick and Boroughmuir are the others.) The Goldenacre club have been trailblazers off the field in recent seasons, with their pioneering sponsorship by Scottish Life. Yet, they have perhaps not done justice to the efforts of their big pack who have seen championship ambitions dashed in the closing stages of the last few seasons. For 1992–93, Heriot's will have a new coaching team, Ian Barnes, the former Hawick international lock, having stood down. John Foster, who in his playing days was a favourite at Gala, will be looking after the backs, while that durable prop, Gregor MacDonald, will be detailed to assist the forwards. Heriot's traditional fluent 15-man game seems certain to be revived by Foster, rugby master at Dollar Academy, one of Scotland's most prolific nurseries which in recent seasons has moulded players such as Cameron Glasgow and John Robertson. Last season, Foster masterminded Dollar's most successful period in their 120-year history and it seems likely that individuals who have completed their schooling may wish to renew acquaintances with their coach in Edinburgh. Heriot's were also fortified by a summer tour of Canada, where Glasgow was deployed in the pivot berth in all four games, reportedly with some success.

Boroughmuir, champions in 1990–91 were at their most enigmatic last season, when they toiled to find the right blend in the backs and were, at one point, on the fringe of the relegation area. Despite his retirement from the international arena, Sean Lineen, happily, remains on duty at Meggetland, where much will be expected of Murry Walker and new recruit Derek Stark (ex-Ayr). Stand-off Walker toured Japan with Scotland in 1989 and showed signs last year of having rediscovered the form which interested the national selectors. One problem exercising coach Bruce Hay will be to unearth a replacement for giant Kiwi, Mark Cooksley, who went on to feature in the All Blacks squad touring Australia and South Africa after his stint at Meggetland.

Currie won many admirers last season for the exciting brand of rugby they played and in captain Ally Donaldson, they have one of the most astute stand-offs in the division. They have lost one of their New Zealand contingent, Grant Nolan, for this year's campaign, but hope to have another, lock Murray Laugerson, making a reappearance. Their back-row forward, Bruce Ward, who has won Edinburgh honours, spent the summer playing in New Zealand and his experience under the new laws is certain to be tapped by coach Graham Hogg, who believes the amendments could favour sides with lighter, more mobile forwards.

Watsonians, having finished in mid-table on their return to the First Division, will have the Hastings brothers, Gavin and Scott, as the backbone of their back line and ought also to be able to exploit the pace of Fergus Henderson, a member of the Scottish Students World Cup squad, and the precocious skill of Derrick Lee. In the forwards, Scott Aitken and Murray Rudkin both saw service in Italy during the summer and, under coach Paul Hogarth, are unlikely to deviate from their habitual animated approach.

In the Borders, Kelso's promotion brings the district's representation in the First Division up to six. The Poynder Park side are continuing to nurture some promising prospects as evinced by the success of Kelso Harlequins, but as former international flanker John Jeffrey remarked during the close season, they will face an arduous campaign, especially in the set pieces. The White Shark will captain the club this season, giving assistance to such redoubtable back-row exponents as Clive Millar, Stuart Bennet and Adam Roxburgh.

Gala, after beginning and ending last season with a flourish, will have to fill the vacancy at full-back created by Peter Dods' retiral, the full-back having taken up the position of coach. Malcolm Changleng shaped encouragingly in that role last season, though Michael Dods, who toured North America with Scotland in 1991, might revert to the position. Gala's front-row, consisting of Gary Isaac, captain Ian Corcoran (who was capped as a replacement on Scotland's summer tour), and Hamish Hunter, are one of the best in the Scottish club sphere but much will depend on the good health of their second row, Graham Shepherd and John Laing, and the further maturing of Gregor

Townsend at stand-off.

Selkirk are capable of playing the most attractive rugby but have been hit by a succession of cruel injuries in recent years. Scott Nichol should have recovered from an ankle break to again bring his pace to bear in the backs, but it might be Christmas before Graham Marshall is in a position to contemplate a comeback after his knee ligament damage.

Allan Goodfellow will resume coaching duties at Jed-Forest, another team bedevilled by injury to key personnel last season, though hopefully both the inspirational Gary Armstrong at scrum-half, and loose head prop, Neil McIlroy, will be fit for the fray.

Hawick almost relinquished their place among the élite last season, their key results being victories over Edinburgh Academicals and old rivals, Gala. It was a gruelling season for their international trio, Greig Oliver, Derek Turnbull and Tony Stanger, who all eventually found themselves out of favour with the national selectors. Batteries recharged, and with the foundations in place to keep the flame burning with the town's youth, Hawick are unlikely to face such trauma again, especially given the coaching abilities of Derrick Grant and Jim Renwick.

Glasgow's ambassadors in the First Division remain GHK and Stirling County. The former have an array of forward resources which in the past has made it difficult for players such as Scotland under-21 captain, Andy Ness, to win a regular first XV berth. Behind, there are similar rich pickings led by new captain, Cammy Little. Winger Graham Agnew, a Glasgow policeman, might also be expected

Nicol, Ma'am (The Scotsman)

to make representative impact this season, having made a good impression following his switch from Kilmarnock. Stirling County, one of the first clubs to devote considerable energies to their youth structure, had their premier harvest during the summer. Kenny Logan's debut against Australia in the second Test gave the club their first fully-fledged international. Logan is likely to be fielded at

full-back this season, though Calum Mac-Donald, a prodigious points gatherer who summered in New Zealand, cannot be discounted automatically. In the forwards, there is a surfeit of craft in the back row, where Gareth Flockhart looms as another potential cap aspirant.

Making their First Division debut will be Dundee HSFP, a most welcome addition,

Family affair. Wigtownshire RFC back row – Robert, Dougie, Davie, Alan and John Drysdale;
front row – Andy and Alastair Hose, John and Hugh Parker (The Scotsman)

creating a focal point for rugby outwith the central belt and the Borders. The Mayfield club may find the back five of their pack the area of most consequence in their bid to retain their hard-fought status, as their front row bears all the hallmarks of solidity. Coached by David Leslie and with the likes of Scotland under-19 international Alastair Graham, a possibility for promotion into the back row, Dundee have the backs, energised by Scotland scrum-half, Andy Nicol, to win games, provided they are supplied with possession.

Much entertainment lies in store outwith the First Division. Stewart's-Melville, with their coterie of gifted young backs, will encounter the same difficulties which befell Gala and Watsonians before them, as they endeavour to bounce straight back into the top flight, a target which will strike a chord with West of Scotland. Elsewhere in the Second Division, Glasgow Academicals showed at the tail-end of last season, with their display in Hong Kong and in their own sevens tournament that they are worth rather more than mid-table security, while there will be more than idle curiosity to see how the two promoted teams, Grangemouth and Clarkston, both renowned for their youth policies, fare.

The advance of areas which for too long have been dormant in rugby circles is detectable in many of the divisions. The south-west of Scotland, where the SRU has deployed Graham Kilgour as Youth Development Officer, will see Wigtownshire look to expand on their seventh spot in the Second Division last season, while more, too, might be anticipated from Dumfries in Division Three and Stewartry, promoted as champions from Division Five last season.

One difficulty facing many ambitious clubs in the lower reaches is how they deal with players of promise and whether they should resist a parochial view and encourage such rare ability to find new and more demanding tests. That dilemma has faced Trinity Academicals, relegated to Division Four last season, having lost the likes of Scotland under-21 prop, Ross McNulty, to neighbouring clubs. It's easy to argue as an outsider that a club should be magnanimous about such matters and pinpoint examples of players, having fulfilled their own careers, returning to the club which gave them their start. The corollary, of course, is that the seepage could see the club lose its position, standards might slip and the chances of producing a player of similar potential recede. It is here, perhaps, that clubs should follow the template laid down in Hawick and Gala over many years, where the junior clubs act as feeders. National leagues have played their part in promoting local rivalry and interest. Their raison d'etre, in my view, however, must be to ensure a successful national team. If the choice is playing second fiddle to an age-old foe, or extinction, what would your club decide?

THE DISTRICTS RESTORED

The McEwan's Inter-District Championship Returns With a Full Programme

Harry Pincott

IN THE SEASON of the Rugby World Cup, the 1991–92 McEwan's Inter-District Championship was a truncated affair with no overall winner, Scotland using the half dozen or so games that did take place to prepare their players for the sterner tests that lay ahead.

This season, however, the Championship returns in its full glory and whether the clubs like it or not – and many of them don't – they are going to have to get on without their top players for two Saturdays in November and the first half of December. One can understand the clubs' frustrations because after the first batch of league fixtures they hardly see their leading performers until the next league outing, usually sometime in January, squeezed in between the international trial and the first Five Nations Championship game. But there's no doubt that the Scottish Rugby Union still view the District Championship as an integral part of their programme, introducing the better players to a higher standard of rugby in preparation for an even higher step up to international level. And as that standard appears to get higher each season we simply must give our poten-

tial caps every possible chance of playing with and against each other if we are to compete against the likes of Australia, New Zealand, France, and England.

In order to make the District Championship more competitive and create greater interest in it, the sponsors to their credit have introduced Best Player Awards for each game, while the side who scores most tries – a target usually set by Tony Belfield, managing director of Scottish Brewers – are also suitably rewarded. So with Scotland's best players on parade, the sponsors' incentives, and the opportunity for younger players to make a name for themselves, there's no earthly reason why the Championship should not produce more attractive and competitive games.

By the time the first matches come along on 21 November, when Edinburgh meet Glasgow, and the North and Midlands take on the South, the players, referees and supporters should have become acquainted with the many new laws, which include the five-point try. That the districts themselves take the Championship seriously is fully demonstrated by their efforts to arrange warm-up games, and the occasional tour, at the start of

JJ takes for the South (The Scotsman)

the season, even at the risk of antagonising clubs who want their top brass for pre-league friendlies.

When Edinburgh won the title three years in a row from 1986–87 to 1988–89, they did so with a great deal of style and panache and with the quality of players at their command there appeared no reason why their successful run should not continue. However, Glasgow stopped the capital from making it four in a row and then it was South

who grabbed the title two years ago. Edinburgh, and none more so than their officials, were stung by some poor displays in those two campaigns and they are determined to recapture the silverware this season.

Uniquely among the districts they have undertaken a programme with a weekend visit to the north of England. What makes Edinburgh's plans more interesting is the fact that they are taking what they term their Development Squad, comprising 17 senior

Where now? Sean Lineen, Edinburgh v Glasgow (The Scotsman*)*

players and 18 under-21s, under the management of Rob Flockhart, the former Edinburgh University, Melrose, Boroughmuir and Corstorphine flanker. On Friday, 4 September, Edinburgh will play Cumbria, followed 24 hours later by an under-21 match against Durham or Northumberland. Then on the Sunday there is a match against Durham. While some of Scotland's tourists to Australia such as the Hastings brothers, Gavin and Scott, and Sean Lineen are unlikely to be asked to make the trip, others like the Boroughmuir prop, Peter Wright, now the proud owner of two caps,

have been invited.

Obviously, one of Edinburgh's top priorities is to find a successor to the inspirational David Sole and among the challengers will be Grant Wilson (Boroughmuir), Gary Kenhard (Heriot's), Ross McNulty (Stewart's-Melville) and possibly Stuart Paul (Heriot's). A boost for the capital should be the return to Raeburn Place of their former captain, Jeremy Richardson, who spent last season in the colours of Glasgow High-Kelvinside. Richardson was in the Edinburgh XV which won the title three times and he is sure to be given a warm welcome by the selectors who won't have Jon Price available: the Boroughmuir captain of last season is stepping into semi-retirement because of business commitments. However, the experience picked up in Australia by Wright and the Heriot's flanker, John Robertson, should help strengthen the capital pack, likely to be led by Kenny Milne. Securing line-out ball could be their biggest problem, with much depending on Andy Macdonald's form.

One imagines the Edinburgh Academicals' winger, Alex Moore, is looking forward to the District Championship more than most, thirsting to prove he's got more to offer than Tony Stanger or the fast developing Kenny Logan (Stirling County) when the national selectors get down to thinking about the Five Nations Championship. While Gavin Hastings and Sean Lineen are going to be available this season – Hastings could well take over the captaincy from Sole, and not just at district level – much thought must be given to encouraging younger players to challenge for their places. If Mike Allingham gets over his back problem, which prevented him from doing much bowling during the cricket season, he will challenge Derek Patterson for the scrum berth, with Douglas Wyllie, Ally Donaldson and Murry Walker vying for the scrum-half berth. Other young backs such as Derek Lee (Watsonians), Duncan Macrae (Boroughmuir) and Kenny Milligan (Stewart's-Melville) are likely to be included in the Development Squad.

When one looks back at Edinburgh's successes in the late 1980s, achieved under the coaching of Douglas Morgan, they were the result of team spirit, a commodity that seemed to disappear in the following two seasons. It will now be up to coaches Bruce Hay (Boroughmuir) and Paul Hogarth (Watsonians) to rediscover that spirit, something both are well capable of doing. Both were very much team players at heart during their careers, as were the under-21 coaches, Graham Hogg (Currie) and Ian Barnes. With four such rugby-wise men in charge, Edinburgh should be capable of mounting a serious challenge for the title. Too often in the past they have failed to play to their potential and an opening game against Glasgow should bring out the best in them.

There's little doubt the Edinburgh selectors, among them Jimmy Craig, the former Heriot's centre, are anxious to give their team a higher profile and fitness programmes are likely to be sent to members of the Development Squad. Edinburgh are only too well aware that New Zealand visit Britain next year and four of their games are scheduled for north of the Border. The capital would like nothing better than to lower the tourists' colours, but in order for that to happen a lot of work has to be put in, starting with the visit to the north of England and then right through the District Championship. Considering that Edinburgh have been able to call on such as the Hastings brothers, Alex Moore, Sean Lineen, Douglas Wyllie, Alex Brewster, David Sole, Kenny Milne, Iain Milne and Jim and Finlay Calder, in recent years they should really have done a lot better.

One supposes that would also apply to the South, who have had an abundance of Scottish caps to select from. And like the capital they will start their campaign without one of their leading lights of the last decade or so, the incomparable Peter Dods. The Gala full-back played his last game on the Australian tour and Melrose's Craig Redpath will no doubt be favourite to take over the no. 15 jersey when the South kick off their season with a friendly against those popular Irish visitors, Leinster, on Thursday 3 September.

Assuming that he is still with Melrose, and Scottish rugby as a whole trusts that will be the case, Craig Chalmers could be poised to take the captaincy. If he proves a success then he could well be given the same responsibility in the Scotland XV. Chalmers will emerge as a key man in a South back division which could well be dominated by Melrose, who are likely to provide the centres in Graham Shiel and Derek Bain, and, as already mentioned, Redpath at full-back. And the much underrated Andy Purves could challenge for a place on the left wing though he faces a stiff hurdle in Iwan Tukalo, who is expected to have one last season with Selkirk and the South before, as he has always promised, playing out his career with Royal High, who could certainly do with him.

The great imponderable about the South this season will be the fitness of Gary Armstrong, whose knee injury cost him dear in terms of domestic and international rugby. As well as missing the Five Nations games he had to stay at home as the Scots struggled Down Under. Armstrong's absence allowed Andy Nicol to grab the no. 9 jersey and there's no doubt the Dundee HSFP player has been an outstanding success for his country. But make no mistake, Armstrong wants the jersey back and the District Championship will be the ideal vehicle for him to

prove to the national selectors that he is back to his best.

While the South do not appear to be as well endowed up front as they are behind the scrum, the emergence of Carl Hogg, the tall Melrose back-row player, will be a bonus as will the experience picked up by the Gala hooker, Ian Corcoran. In many peoples' opinion Derek Turnbull should have been in Australia and the Hawick flanker will no doubt choose the District Championship to hammer home that point. Doddie Weir will be the main provider of line-out ball and it's hard to believe the lock is still only 21, such has been the improvement in his play at international level over the past season. Gala's Gary Isaac and Steven Ferguson of Peebles are likely to be first choice props, but if Neil McIlroy (Jed-Forest) regains full fitness he will challenge for a place.

At the time of writing the South have not yet appointed a coach to succeed Alan Goodfellow, who has stood down, but there's no lack of contenders. In addition, Keith Robertson and Roy Laidlaw will be available to help with the backs. The South are away to the North and Midlands in their first Championship match – the venues for all matches have still to be decided – and the composition of the North XV will largely depend on how many of their Edinburgh-based players stay loyal to them.

The new Scotland cap, Rob Wainwright, played for the red-shirted North last season as did his Edinburgh Academicals colleagues, Rowen Sheppard, John Thomson, Rod Mitchell and fellow international David McIvor. No doubt Edinburgh will have asked Wainwright and McIvor at least

GHK v Watsonians (The Scotsman*)*

to change their allegiance but in the interests of a competitive championship it is to be hoped they stay with the North.

Their coach at Raeburn Place, Bob Easson, will be in charge again and they could well have three warm-up matches against Irish side Connacht and Howe of Fife in a game to mark the opening of the club's £100,000 renovations of dressing-rooms, showers etc at Duffus Park. In addition the North officials hope to play Edinburgh Borderers on the Monday before the South game in a repeat of last year's fixture. With Andy Nicol at scrum-half and Martin Scott at hooker, North could field four caps and while their victories are few and far between they are always capable of springing a surprise. Just ask the Anglo-Scots, who lost to the North a couple of years ago. To the dismay of the victors, the bar ran out of beer. And so did the plane on the way back.

The Anglos have made a notable contribution since coming into the District Championship and it has allowed players like Damian Cronin, Chris Gray, Ian Smith, Peter Jones, Lindsay Renwick and Paul Burnell, to mention a few, to further their representative careers. Derek White was, of course, a cap before he joined London Scottish. Unfortunately for them, the Anglos will be missing the inspirational no. 8, who will be playing club rugby only this season, but with Jones, Gray, Cronin and Smith available they have the nucleus of a very strong pack. It is not yet known if Burnell's knee injury will have healed in time and there's no way the prop will be rushing back too soon. Though David Millard had an unhappy tour he is a very good player and he and backs like Mark Appleson and Fraser Harrold will provide the Anglos with the right players in the key positions.

With both David Leslie and David Kirk not available, the Anglos will be looking for a new coaching team, not an easy job for anyone, given how far spread the players are. No warm-up matches have yet been arranged for a team who will cram their four district games into ten days, including two mid-week outings. As a spokesman said, 'We just have to press on and make the most of it', and to their credit, the Anglos have certainly done that. They make enormous sacrifices to take part in the Championship and deserve any success they get. One of their mid-week dates heralds their first outing, against Glasgow, somewhere in England. The Glasgow side, coached by David Johnston (Watsonians) and Hugh Campbell (Edinburgh Academicals), will have already played Edinburgh and the South by the time they take on the Anglos and that must give them a huge advantage.

Glasgow, like the South, play a warm-up game against Leinster, on 5 September, and various squad sessions have been arranged, including under-21 get-togethers which should provide the selectors with plenty of players to choose from. The new Scotland cap, Kenny Logan, from Stirling County, will be sure of a place, either at full-back or on the wing, while Derek Stark and Alan Watt should be in good fettle after their Australian experiences. After having been passed by Peter Wright as Burnell's deputy in the Scotland XV, Watt could well decide that a return to second row, which in my opinion

is his best position, could improve his fortunes. Stirling County's Brian Ireland should be fit to reclaim his wing-forward berth alongside the likes of Fergus Wallace (Glasgow High-Kelvinside), Jim Brough (Stirling County) and David McVey (Ayr) and Glasgow's biggest problem could be finding a pair of half-backs.

One hopes they do because it's important that Glasgow, and the other sides, field full-strength XVs and make the District Championship a truly competitive and meaningful affair.

DISTRICT CHAMPIONSHIPS PROGRAMME
(Venues still to be decided)

November 21: Edinburgh v Glasgow
North and Midlands v South

November 28: North and Midlands v Edinburgh
Glasgow v South

December 2: Anglo-Scots v Glasgow

December 5: South v Anglo-Scots
Glasgow v North and Midlands

December 9: Edinburgh v Anglo-Scots

December 12: South v Edinburgh
Anglo-Scots v North and Midlands

White all the way (The Scotsman)

The Royal Bank of Scotland

HAIL AND FAREWELL

A Tribute to the Retiring Scottish Internationals

Derek Douglas

HAIL AND FAREWELL. It's been a good old, bad old season for international departures. Just gone, but assuredly not forgotten, after the Australian tour are David Sole, Peter Dods and Sean Lineen. Derek White had already called it a day after the Five Nations Championship. The previous October, at the conclusion of Scotland's fourth-place World Cup campaign, John Jeffrey and Finlay Calder had hung up their international boots. At the end of the same tournament, coaches Jim Telfer and Derrick Grant retired from the international scene after nearly a decade of sterling service to Scottish rugby.

Scotland's international set-up will absorb these losses, of course it will. No one is indispensable. Others will step forward to fill the vacant boots and Scottish rugby will continue to prosper. But there is no denying that with the departure from the international stage of so many class acts, the Scottish game will be the poorer and the Murrayfield crowd will be denied further sight of performances which have stirred the blood and set the terracings ablaze.

And talking of Murrayfield terracings; we must record, too, the transient nature of bricks and mortar. The bulldozers and pile-drivers moved in after Scotland's last home game of the Five Nations season against France. By the start of the 1993 international season the North and South ends at Murrayfield will boast covered stands, the first phase of a multi-million pound development which will completely revamp the ground and provide a stadium fit to take Scottish rugby into the 21st century and beyond.

But it is not from bricks, mortar and concrete that rugby memories are fashioned. Rugby is about players. It is about courage, commitment, nerve and style. It is about extraordinary sporting endeavour which rises above the humdrum and deposits a memory trace which will burn bright until the day we shuffle off this mortal coil. And each of the departees has enriched our collective store of sporting memories by their contribution to the national cause.

David Sole, Grand Slam captain courageous. Was there ever a more athletically gifted prop-forward? He had cricketer's hands, a devastating turn of pace and tackled like the clap of doom. Given the right personnel behind him he was always a much better scrummager than his critics gave him

Spider man Finlay Calder (The Scotsman)

Sad end – JJ's last appearance at Murryfield (The Scotsman)

credit for. His performances during the victorious British Lions' tour to Australia in 1989 when he was first-choice loose-head prop in all three Tests proved that. But it is for his dynamic play in the loose and for his inspirational leadership that Sole will be most remembered.

David Michael Barclay Sole, holder of 44 caps, captained Scotland a record 25 times, overhauling the record set by another loose-head skipper, Ian McLauchlan, against England in 1992. Sole's leadership skills were recognised elsewhere, too. As Finlay Calder's lieutenant, he captained the British Lions twice in 1989. Additionally, he skippered the Barbarians on numerous occasions and in 1992 captained a world invitation side to a rare victory over the All Blacks during the New Zealand Rugby Union's centenary season.

Sole's quiet off-field demeanour belied a fearsome commitment and desire to win. The gladiatorial nature of his slow and menacing march on to the Murrayfield turf before the 1990 Grand Slam showdown against England has entered rugby folklore. With his trademark white headband, Sole was never difficult to pick out. Invariably, though, such a recognition aid would not be required. Look to where the action was hottest and there would be Sole, body language screaming belligerent defiance. He entered the side along with five other debutants in 1986 and thereafter, save for a nose and cheek injury which meant he was sidelined for three international matches, he was a permanent fixture in the Scotland side.

He was just 30 when he retired at an age when most prop forwards, like good wine,

are maturing to perfection. It wasn't, though, the registration number which had most influenced his decision to call it a day after the Australian tour. Sole had played at the top, first with Bath and the Anglos and then with Edinburgh Academicals, Edinburgh, Scotland and the British Lions, for almost a decade. It was, he said, the mileage on the body clock which had been the overriding factor leading to retirement. The time had come to devote more of his time to family and business. Unbelievably, there were those who had reckoned that since he had already announced his retirement, Sole should have been excluded from the 1992 Australian tour. It was the stamp of the man that he had made himself available in the first place. It was always going to be hard. The Wallabies were the world champions after all and Scotland were a side in transition. Sole could have bowed out at the end of the Five Nations Championship. He had nothing further to prove. However, with a young touring party under his wing he viewed the trip as a challenge and his inspirational leadership qualities were never shown in better light than when he came on as a substitute against the Emerging Wallabies and Scotland turned a 4–24 deficit into a face-saving 24-all draw. Then, in defeat during the Second Test in Sydney, his personal performance shone like a burning beacon and was rewarded with a try – his third in a Scotland jersey.

David Sole could have played for England. There is little doubt that he would indeed have played for the Auld Enemy had he not achieved his lifetime desire to play for Scotland. He had, in fact, appeared with some success in an England under-23 trial match but before selection for England under-23 could occur he had written to Murrayfield asking at what point his boats would be burned so far as Scotland were concerned. His grandfather was Scottish and the family stayed in Aberdeenshire. He had gone to school in Scotland – Blairmore and Glenalmond – and had played for Scottish Schools. Subsequently, he worked his way through Scotland B and won his first cap against the French at Murrayfield in 1986, that match being most memorable for the opening seconds try by the Tricolors' scrum-half Pierre Berbizier. The Scots overcame this early setback to win 18–17 and Sole's international career was launched on a victorious note. His untimely retirement leaves a massive void, both in the front row and in terms of the captaincy. It serves, too, as a warning for for future. The playing and extra-curricular demands now being made of international rugby players will assuredly lead to more early retirements. Players of Sole's calibre will be lost to the game in their prime. We will all be the losers.

Calder, White and Jeffrey. Like a long-established firm of family solicitors, the three names belonged together. They were the Old Firm of Scottish rugby and whenever they were on duty the international side's efforts revolved around them. That this was indeed the case is evidenced by the fact that by the time of the 1991 World Cup, for which Calder had been coaxed out of retirement, the Scottish side boasted no fewer than 19 back-row moves. The Calder-White-Jeffrey axis was used as a belligerent platform from which to launch strikes deep into the heart of enemy territory. Individually they were

impressive. As a unit the Three Musketeers ruled supreme.

Derek White was the senior partner having earned the first of his 41 caps as a flanker against France in 1982. He suffered, though, from his sheer versatility. He could, and did, play in the second row, at wing-forward and at no. 8, his preferred berth. He went on, despite stern competition from John Beattie and Iain Paxton, to play 29 times for Scotland in the no. 8 shirt and to become Scotland's most capped no. 8 forward and a British Lion to boot. Shy and unassuming but with a dry sense of humour, White was ever the quiet man in the Scottish back row. But Fin and JJ more than made up for that! He was, too, a notable try-scorer. He notched a hat-trick against Wales three years ago and with a total of 11 international tries to his name he holds, with John Jeffrey, the record for a Scottish forward.

Despite advancing years – he was 34 – White saved some of the best rugby of his career for his swansong season. He was the pick of the pack against Ireland at Lansdowne Road and in his final Murrayfield appearance against France he pulled off a try-saving tackle on Franck Mesnel when it seemed that the French centre must score. He was never a flamboyant player but Derek Bolton White will be sorely missed.

Next in seniority came John Jeffrey. The media dubbed him the White Shark but his team-mates just called him JJ. He and Finlay Calder decided that enough was enough after the World Cup third and fourth place play-off match against the All Blacks in Cardiff. Jeffrey was 32 and with 40 international appearances to his name, he remains Scot-

Front row union: David Sole and Burnell (The Scotsman)

land's most capped flanker. Making light of
the asthma from which he suffered – a
complaint shared with Derek White – JJ
seemingly possessed the ability to run all day.
It would be a tragedy if he were to be most
remembered for the damage inflicted on the
Calcutta Cup after the 1988 game against
England. But he won't be. He was too good a
player for that. A la Jean-Pierre Rives, his
blond locks made him instantly recognisable
on the field of play and, like the Frenchman,
JJ would invariably be first to the breakdown
point, first with the tackle and first to lead the
charge back upfield.

And then came Fin. Irrepressible Fin.
Ever optimistic Fin. Ruthless Fin. Finlay
Calder OBE came late to international
rugby. The career of twin brother Jim was
over by the time that Finlay forced his way
into the side in 1986 along with David Sole,
the Hastings brothers, Matt Duncan and
Jeremy Campbell-Lamerton. Raw-boned
and long-striding, Finlay Calder seemed to
eat up the yards as he charged upfield with,
more often than not, the ball held in one
hand. One incident from all of the others, for
me, sums up his illustrious career. It came in
the 1990 Grand Slam decider against
England. He gathered up a loose ball and
charged straight at the English pack. Micky
Skinner got in a big hit but Calder absorbed
the crunching tackle and stayed on his feet
until the Scottish pack arrived en masse and
drove him upfield before England conceded
the penalty which put Scotland on the road to
victory. Later, with victory secured, Calder
offered the hand of friendship to a disconso-
late Brian Moore. That was the mark of the
man.

Aw, Dad: Jamie and David Sole
(*The* Scotsman)

Calder captained Scotland in 1989. That
summer he captained, too, the British Lions
in Australia. It was a trial by fire. The first
Test was lost, and lost badly. Calder needed
all of his leadership abilities to drag the
touring party out of the depths of despair and
to secure victory in the second Test a week
later. He took a pounding from the Australian media and from some sections of the
British press who were calling for his head.
But the second Test was won and the series
secured with a fine victory in the decider at
Sydney. On his return he took an early
season sabbatical and for the 1990 championship season the captaincy passed to his good
friend David Sole. Calder played out of his
skin throughout that Grand Slam season and
on the summer tour to New Zealand after
which he 'retired' only to be coaxed out of
retirement for the 1991 World Cup competi-

tion by coach Ian McGeechan. It was, said Calder, 'pay back time', a reference to the debt which the British Lion felt was owed to McGeechan who had coached the 1989 tourists in Australia.

By now Calder was almost 34 and a hard summer of training saw him fit enough to offer himself for inclusion in the final World Cup squad. His last sojourn on the world stage was not without controversy. A hard tackle on the Irish full-back Jim Staples brought accusations that he had utilised a fore-arm jab. Calder received 'hate mail' from aggrieved Irishmen and this upset him greatly. I have on my study wall a wonderful photograph of Calder in full flight during the 1990 Murrayfield game against the French. He has the ball cradled in his right hand. The left arm is flailing and the legs are pumping as he breenges for the line with three Frenchmen in hot pursuit. A Gallic cockerel, all feet and feathers, is frantically flapping to get out of the way. That is how we will remember Calder.

Finally, no tribute to Finlay Calder can be complete without reference to the humour of the man. Calder stories are myriad. My favourite, true or apocryphal I care not, concerns an incident during a sevens tournament in Australia in 1988. Calder, in an invitation side which was playing the All Blacks, had just pole-axed the Kiwi winger John Kirwan with a tackle that was, to give it the benefit of the doubt, 'marginal'. 'That was a bit late,' said the big Aucklander. Calder, mindful of the 'lip' that Kirwan had given to the Scots during their World Cup meeting the previous year, observed wrily: 'Aye, about a year too bloody late!'

Peter Dods was the ultimate team player. He bridged the Andy Irvine-Gavin Hastings full-back era. Some bridge, some era! He was too, a Grand Slam hero. He was on the bench throughout 1990 until an injury before the Calcutta Cup showdown with England robbed him of full participation in the weekend's glorious events. He was there, though, as an honoured guest. The team had insisted. But if his participation in the 1990 Grand Slam had been in the role of onlooker then in 1984 he had been a full-blooded competitor. His contribution to that 1984 campaign was immense and not just on account of the 50 points he scored in that championship season.

Peter Dods was slightly built but as brave as the Lion he was. Remember how, like a prize-fighter, he finished the climactic game against Jean-Pierre Rives's rattled Frenchmen with an eye bruised and shut tight. Remember, too, how he refused to allow the facial damage to affect his defensive fielding work or his goal-kicking. Dods the faithful servant participated in 12 overseas tours in 13 years. He was a prodigious gatherer of points. His goal-kicking prowess was evident right up until his final appearance for Scotland, against Queensland, during the Australian tour. Fittingly, he led the side and kicked three penalty goals and two conversions during the 12–29 win. That afternoon's haul in Toowoomba raised Dods's career tour total to 448. The younger members of the touring party with black good humour called him Zimmer in recognition of his 34 summers. They also called him The Legend. With the international shadows of first Irvine and then Hastings hanging over him, Peter Dods still managed to amass 23 caps. Dods may have retired but The Legend lives on.

Sean Raymond Patrick Lineen, the Kiwi Scot with the Irish moniker, was a revelation when he burst on to the Scottish club scene with Boroughmuir. Endowed with a visionary sixth sense and by virtue of the highly productive angles that he ran, Lineen carved open hitherto solid defences with apparent ease. He qualified to wear the thistle on account of a Hebridean grandfather and earned the first of his 29 caps against Wales in 1989. He established a lucrative midfield partnership with Scott Hastings with whom he has set up a Test-centre-duo world record. Personable and easy-going off the field, Lineen's Kiwi pedigree shone through in his never-say-die attitude on it. His father, Terry, was capped 12 times by the All Blacks and family loyalties must have been strained to the limit when Sean returned to his native New Zealand as a member of the Grand Slam winning Scotland side which played a summer series against the All Blacks. Lineen has taken his adopted country to heart. He has a good Scots lass for a fiancée and it is their intention to marry and settle in Edinburgh.

Finally, it would be remiss indeed not to close this tribute to the departing stars without marking the tremendous debt owed by Scottish rugby to two of the back-room boys who departed after the World Cup. Jim Telfer and Derrick Grant, both Borderers, back-row forwards and British Lions in their playing days, each contributed massively to Scottish rugby throughout the eighties and into the nineties. This was, arguably, the most successful period ever in the history of the Scottish game and Telfer and Grant, in their coaching capacities, have had more than a little to do with that success.

Both were men who did not suffer fools gladly, or at all. They were dedicated to the cause of Scottish rugby almost to the point of obsession. Both were involved during the 1990 Grand Slam campaign. For Telfer it was a case of déjà vu. He had been principal coach to the 1984 Grand Slam winning side. Just as Grant had coached his native Hawick side to a series of Scottish championships, Telfer coached Melrose to a brace of championship wins. Both are still involved with their club sides. They are coaches out of the top drawer and they will be sorely missed.

Hail and farewell, then, to them all. Each in his way has contributed a chapter to the story of Scottish rugby. But that story is an ongoing tale of high endeavour, selfless commitment, raw courage, soaring success and, sometimes, grinding disappointment. New faces will appear to fill the void left by the departed ones. Some of the debutants might even become stars in their own right. One cannot help thinking, though, that we have been privileged to witness the end of a rugby era. We thank them all for the enjoyment that they have provided for those of us on the Murrayfield terracings and in the stands. It's been a pleasure to know you.

With a little help from a friend: Greig Oliver and Craig Chalmers
(The Scotsman)

WAITING IN THE WINGS

Scotland's Emerging Internationals

John Beattie

JUST AS THE sun sets gracefully at the end of a frenetic day, and yet rises afresh in the morning mist to give us hope for the hours to come, so each international rugby player's career is but a flash on the history board of the sport with his position to be taken gladly by someone younger and fresher when selectors, arthritis, or a combination of injuries and old age make his exit from international rugby inevitable. How often in the middle eighties did we hear the cry 'What on earth are we going to do without ... Colin Deans ... or ... Rutherford and Laidlaw ... or ... Iain Milne ... or ... Alan Tomes ...' Indeed the list could go on forever if we go back to the Carmichaels, Browns, Irvines and the rest of their generation. Throughout rugby history the one, sure, unarguable fact that has arisen is that there *will* be a replacement found for the supposedly irreplaceable player. The newcomer, extremely unfortunate indeed for the person on the way out, may even end up more than a match for such a recent and cherished memory. The day that there are more famous names in the press box, as it has been in Wales for about ten years, is the day that we should all just chuck it in.

The other side of the coin is that there is a tendency to regard current Scottish squads more highly than their predecessors because they are better coached and have more opportunities to practise together. But to deny the true greats of the past their real worth would be grossly unfair, as it would be to try to name a few examples but John Rutherford, famous for once leaving five opponents sitting on their backsides scratching their heads in amazement on his way to a try, would just have to be one.

But as the recent tour to Australia demonstrated, it isn't inconceivable that relatively good club players end up full international caps before the rest of the country really expects them to and, as has been said so many times before, we are in an era that is seeing the greatest mass retiral of players that has ever occurred. The real problem may be that the side to disappear between the World Cup, and now, had more than its fair share of class even to the outsider, and Calder, Jeffrey, Sole, Lineen, White, Milne, and those that will inevitably follow, have to be replaced right now. Any perceived phasing-in can't occur because of lack of time, and those that have already made it to full cap status will be building on a tour that was as unsuccessful as any undertaken by Scotland in it's recent history – partly because of the

Coach David Johnston learning how to tackle at the hands of his former captain (The Scotsman)

sheer quality of the opposition, and partly, it has to be said, because of the quality of the Scottish squad in world terms. Peter Wright, who stuck superbly to his task and put the boot in as required, Martin Scott, Carl Hogg, Ian Corcoran and Kenny Logan have all had the call and therefore have to be omitted from any article on future international players in the future sense. But if motivation was ever needed for players on the fringes of international selection, then a scan through that batch of players is a must for others who wish to tread a similar path.

For much of the season Peter Wright was languishing a good five yards behind play, arriving late in English forward driving position (*circa* 1986), and looking for all the world like a man ill at ease in the game of rugby. So much so that even his admirers at

his club were starting to worry about his attitude. Then came selection for the tour. For me, his was the performance to note, for despite struggling in the set pieces and arriving in Australia after a season of mediocrity with a club that also looked off-colour, he rampaged against far bigger opponents and refused to bow down. Anybody with that kind of steel deserves a great deal of respect, save for the needless arguing with referees. Whether he can continue to improve and get down to the graft in another domestic season will be fascinating to watch, and with Paul Burnell's expected return from injury, only Peter Wright has any real control over his future cap prospects. Martin Scott, who has already played in a side that beat Scotland in their World Cup warm-up, was probably everybody's bet for a cap eventually, but the manner in which he ultimately received it, when poor Ian Corcoran was dumped, certainly brought home the fact that there is no room in rugby for those of thin skin. Few can imagine the thoughts that must have been floating in Corcoran's head when he was told, you have to assume privately, that his promotion to the big team was not to be automatic. Sadder still when you consider that there were those in the Australian side that thought Corcoran the more awkward player.

When so much of a player's reputation among his peers is made on hard tours, with both on- and off-field conduct taken into account, it's difficult to tell whether Kenny Logan and Carl Hogg have risen to the status of permanent future cap contenders in the long term. Both must realise that necessity may have to be the watchword as there have

Armstrong in action (The Scotsman)

always been perceived weaknesses on the wings and Gavin Hastings can't go on forever. In Hogg's favour is the fact that he has both height and bulk to present to an area of the scrum that has seen both disappear in one fell swoop – the back row.

Having spoken about the fine gentlemen above, a logical way to proceed is to have a look at what the country needs in the way of future international players, and then fire a few names about. It should be remembered that we are in a generation-skipping process which will see the selectors blooding some players that would not have been considered ready in the olden days, when Scotland gained a reputation for being very faithful to its teams: few players made the international side at the same youthful stage as some All Blacks or, especially, the Australians. We're now talking of some very young future caps,

Wainwright takes French (The Scotsman)

but if they're good enough when they're young, then why not? Perhaps the Scots will start having under-21 tours in the style of the Emerging Wallabies and the New Zealand Rugby News youth side that has been to America among other places.

Taking the front row first. David Sole has gone forever and everyone you speak to seems to await in fear the consequences for the Scottish team. A man who can make things go backwards when he runs into them, can hove to in the scrummage with the best,

and still has the energy to run around like a spring chicken is, therefore, urgently sought. Or someone better, though that's highly unlikely. Peter Jones has had the nod from Sole himself as the heir apparent to the loose-head slot yet still has to convince the watching public, while Iain Milne went as far as to suggest to Alan Watt that he might fare better on the left. However, neither of those two conform to internationally accepted standards as far as top-class loose-head props are concerned. It could be argued that many

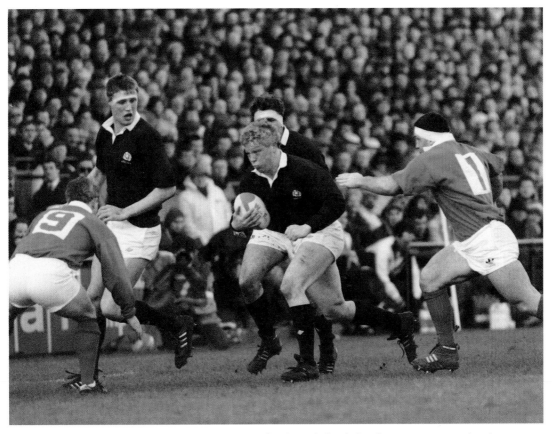

New boys Dave McIvor, Doddie Weir and Neil Edwards lead the charge against Ireland
(*The* Scotsman)

recent Scottish teams were like that. But there's no escaping the fact that modern props are getting more and more in the David Sole mould with bulk. Unfortunately there is nobody of comparable quality playing at the moment. To take people back for a moment, when David Sole broke onto the scene in 1986, the players around him, the selectors, and especially people he happened to run into on the training pitch, all knew he was special and knew he had to make it. There's no one like that today playing in Scotland, although it would be great to go into print and say that there was, and yet someone somewhere will be found and nourished, coaxed and bullied into taking over the great man's mantle.

Perhaps more of an understudy is needed for Kenny Milne who will hopefully be around for some time to come, and Scott and Corcoran are an ideal pair to scrap over that. Crucially in the tight-head slot, Steve Ferguson of Peebles (a son of the soil as Bill McLaren would say) could soon find himself getting some weighted nods. Second row has suddenly become a contentious area with a great deal of height and especially weight being given away until the second Test against Australia and the recall of Damian Cronin. There are indications that a few youngsters are willing and have all the necessary personal qualities, as well as the physical dimensions to give it all a real go. Among them is Murray Rudkin of Watsonians, who just about satisfies the criteria for modern second rows at the highest level, and enjoys putting himself about and a refreshed Shade Munro.

It's behind the second row that the problems start to stand up and hit you in the face. Rob Wainwright has now been capped and has his supporters as captain. Dave McIvor will be up there again barring injury, and there are many who argue that he was unlucky to lose his place in Australia by falling into the age old trap of leaving an awful lot on the training field. Ian Smith has risen in everyone's estimation and with Carl Hogg in the frame this foursome could have a monopoly in the near future unless Darren Burns of Biggar makes a late charge. One complete lowball though is Gordon Mackay of my own club, who, like Iain Jarvie before him, is better pound for pound than any rival he could face in Scotland. However, the coaching hasn't been there, and in many ways he is at the wrong club. It just goes to show that youngsters don't compete on a level playing field when it comes to the pedigree for their caps: there's a vast difference in the knowledge that is being passed down on some Tuesdays in Glasgow when compared to the same process in dark corners

of the Borders, and even Edinburgh now.

Even further backfield, at scrum-half, there is an embarrassment of riches. Andy Nicol and Gary Armstrong have still to blast their final showdown, and there's a third silky performer in 'Deke' Patterson of Edinburgh Accies who has lightning quick hands and could happily replace either of the more famous pair. Patterson, ironically, also played in the game that saw the Edinburgh Borderers beat the national side.

Stand-offs are a special breed, as anybody who can receive hundreds of passes and wilfully kick so much possession away in the name of a game plan needs to be. Craig Chalmers definitely has that air of self belief so needed in a game where wing forwards run past you suggesting the most wicked things. He may have to watch himself though, because if ever Gregor Townsend shrugs off his correspondingly timid air, he will present a serious challenge to Chalmers, despite Chalmers being the only Scots player chosen by Australian Test prop Ewen Mckenzie for his most glamorous current world fifteen. Townsend is in an unusual situation; so many people are willing him on to succeed, for here is a player who, just out of school, was displaying touches on the field of play that were seconds ahead in thought of his team-mates. Ultimately, it may have to be that Chalmers and Townsend both play as each of those remarkable men can win games on their own. We've all seen it too.

Sean Lineen has said he's going, and its hard to forget my own first sight of him in a game against Hawick; all of a sudden, here was a player that could pass, ran straight, looped after passing, and always seemed to

Try again, Finlay (The Scotsman*)*

tackle his man. Lineen caught the eye because players of his quality are rare in domestic rugby. He will be difficult to replace, although one man who should surely have been taken to Australia and wasn't, and has a better physical build than some who were, is Ian Jardine the Stirling County centre. Ask the players who they least like to play against, and Jardine comes near the top of the list. But somehow he didn't make it despite domestic appearances of the highest order, although he should find himself back in the scheme of things if he hasn't lost too much heart. Considering that he was the outstanding player in the national trial, and his B caps, then Jardine has to be a genuine full-cap contender.

In general, being asked to identify the future Scottish caps is a bit like being asked to

Break out: Graham Shiel (The Scotsman)

predict the score on the night before an international. Getting a Scottish cap, even in a period when the level of latent talent may not be at its highest, still demands a level of sacrifice that very few people are willing to face. The first thing that any cap sees is that he is suddenly surrounded by people driven by the same force, who are similarly single-minded, and who cherish the same things in life in a strange way.

Over the next few months a group of youngsters are going to jump through the hoops of the selection process; they will train as they have never done before, turn up for Sunday squad sessions to be tortured by some lunatic of a coach in the driving rain, stay in every Friday night, end up playing in almost meaningless Wednesday night games under the floodlights, and play through at least two bouts of the flu. All this in the distant, magnetic hope that at the end of it will be that one thing that could set them apart from a majority of rugby players ... a cap. The frightening thought is that most of them won't make it. Ah well, such is life.

THE EYES OF THE NEW LAW

Refereeing Under Rugby's New Laws

Jim Fleming

TO REFEREE Australia against New Zealand in a Bledisloe Cup match is a daunting task at the best of times, but to be asked to officiate the same match on 4 July as the first international under new radical law changes filled me with a certain amount of apprehension. As it transpired my apprehension was ill-founded, not because of the laws themselves, although that was part of the answer, but because of the extremely positive way in which the players and coaches had looked at and used the new laws. This was not only the case in the international but in all games that I saw or refereed in Australia.

The alterations to the present laws have come about because of the fact that the game as we know it at present has become so bogged down in a plethora of stoppages, scrummages and penalty kicks at goal, that the proportion of the 80 minutes where the ball is actually in play has become less and less. I would venture to suggest that with the correct attitude and application of the new laws by all, the game of rugby will now benefit enormously. I feel that it is important for us all to look at the new laws with a positive attitude (for example, how best can

we get good, clean, fast ball) rather than look upon the changes from the negative viewpoint (for example, how best can we prevent or disrupt our opponents getting ball). It is obvious from my short time in Australia that the former is the attitude being adopted both in that country and in New Zealand, and that we in the Home nations will be in danger of being left even further behind in the modern game if we do not adopt a similar attitude.

In my opinion the main alterations to the laws which have had the greatest impact on the game in Australia, and will have the most impact on the game in this country, concern those made to the line-out, the ruck and maul, the tackle, and the offside law. Although the other alterations, including the five-point try, have had an impact to a greater or lesser degree, the four that I've noted are the ones which will come into play time and time again and are the ones which I noted from the games in Australia were the most influential.

The new line-out law has been written so that now jumpers stand a better chance of getting an unimpeded jump for the ball, so long as they go for it with two hands or the inside arm. The gap of a metre between both teams should now be looked on as sacrosanct. In Australia, referees were insisting that the gap should be even more than one metre so that players who tried to interfere with the opposition jumpers were easily picked up by the referee. Players who moved towards the line of touch and were not jumping for the ball were immediately penalised with a free kick. Due to the fact that players can now stand closer to players in their own team – the gap between members of the same team is no longer specified in law – it was obvious that players now are more intent on 'assisting' or protecting their jumpers rather than disrupting the opposition. The result being that cleaner, quicker ball was won by all teams instead of the lottery which line-outs have been for years. It must have been obvious to all who watched the Australia v New Zealand match on television that under the new laws more good two-handed catches were taken by all the line-out jumpers due to the fact that they only had to worry about their opposite number and not some prop driving them out of the way, which in previous seasons may or may not have been picked up by the referee.

Although they were not shown on the highlights on British television, there were two or three occasions when a quick throw-in was taken by Australia under the new laws. This meant that the ball was thrown in anywhere from where the ball went into touch and the defender's goal line. The result being that time was not wasted on forming a line-out and the attacking options were increased by the side throwing-in. Again more movement and a more fluid game.

The changes to the ruck and maul law, especially the maul, were the ones over which many people voiced concern. Before refereeing matches under the new laws, I have to admit to being one of those sceptics. Having now watched and refereed this alteration, I am totally convinced that it has been an excellent improvement. The onus is now on the ball-carrier or the team with the ball in its possession to do something with it in the maul otherwise they will eventually lose the put-in at the scrummage. The phrase 'use it or lose it' can now be heard during maul situations in Australia. Although mauls and rolling mauls still exist, and thankfully will continue to exist in our game, the onus is put fairly and squarely on the ball-carrying team to keep the ball alive. There was one point in the international which I refereed in Sydney where the All Blacks rolled a maul some twenty to thirty yards towards the Australian line where it then collapsed, the ball becoming trapped in a heap of bodies. The put-in went to Australia two metres from their own goal line. It looked unfair, but the All Blacks had had ample opportunity to use the ball prior to the collapse and had refused to do so. There were only five occasions during the match when the put-in at the scrummage went to the side not going forward.

The one major difference that this law has made is that there will be fewer scrummages due to the fact that no team wants to get the ball trapped in the maul and so lose possession. Therefore the ball will be kept alive and there will be more movement. The Australia v New Zealand game only had a total of eighteen scrummages (just four in the first half) and only five scrummages for collapsed mauls which is much fewer than in previous seasons.

The tackle law is a change which I think should suit the game in Scotland down to the ground. Our game is based on rucking with players on their feet. The law now prevents anybody from going to ground after a tackle, no matter what the location of the ball (except if the ball is in in-goal when players can dive on it to secure a try or touch-down). Problems have arisen over the years as to the referee's interpretation of the distance the ball had to be from a tackle before a player could go to ground. That problem has now been removed: to play the ball after a tackle a player must be on his feet and can now only pick up the ball or play it with his feet. It is unlikely, due to body position and proximity of opponents, that a player will attempt to pick the ball up, and to kick it might be giving the ball back to the opponent. What is now happening in the Southern hemisphere is that players are driving over the ball and leaving it to be picked up by their scrum-half, creating good ruck ball, ideally suited to our game in Scotland. Again because players are not going to deck there are fewer pile-ups and therefore fewer scrums and fewer penalties, making for a quicker game and a game with more movement.

The changes to the offside law have certainly helped the game. No longer will we see players advancing to ten metres of where the ball is to alight and stand there until they are played onside, thereby cutting down the counter-attacking options of the defending player catching the ball, who invariably could only kick it back down the field. Now

On the spot: Jim Fleming well positioned (*The* Scotsman)

if you are in front of the ball when it is kicked you cannot move forward. You must stand still until you are played onside or if you are within ten metres of where the ball is to land you must retire. The result of this alteration, I have found, is that players who catch the ball have more space to move the ball and counter-attack, producing more movement in the game and less aimless kicking back and forward down the pitch.

When a penalty or free kick has been awarded, the team who have the kick now do not have to wait until everybody from their team retires behind the ball. A quick kick or tap can now be taken regardless of whether members of the same team are in front of the ball. I have been surprised how many players took this option in Australia. Not only did they maintain their impetus and forward movement with the ball but they were also able to take advantage of their opponents'

World Cup: Jim Fleming cools temperatures. Ireland v Australia (The Scotsman*)*

inability to regroup their defences.

I am sure that those of you who saw the Australia v New Zealand game on television or read about it in the press were impressed with the way the teams played, the way they adapted to the new law changes, and the general speed and movement of the game. I can assure everybody that this attitude from players was not confined to the international but was in evidence in all the club rugby which I refereed or watched. As our new season begins, the ball is very much in our

court. We have seen how the new laws can make the game far better to play and watch. It will mean that we will have to look at how the game has been played in the past and how we want it to be played in the future. I also believe, from first-hand experience, that to play under the new laws, players and referees will have to be fitter and quicker about the field. The onus is on us all, players, coaches and referees, to approach the new laws in a positive way for the good of the game in Scotland.

The Royal Bank
of Scotland

MAGNIFICENT SEVENS

The Murrayfield World International Sevens

Bill McLaren

THOSE WHO HAVE been fortunate enough to savour the particular delicacy that is the Cathay Pacific and Hong Kong Bank seven-a-side tournament will be in no doubt about the glamorous prospect in store at the World International Sevens at Murrayfield between April 16 and 18 in 1993.

In Hong Kong at the end of March and beginning of April the world brings its sevens squads for a breathtaking extravaganza of good fellowship, celebration and highly competitive sevens play. The Hong Kong event also sets before its enthusiastic and highly responsive audience the sheer wonder of actually seeing such unlikely Rugby Union nations as Sri Lanka, Korea, Singapore, Malaysia, and Papua New Guinea not only playing the short game with flair, skill and participation pleasure but, what is more, squaring up to the heavy-weights, Fiji, New Zealand, Australia, the Barbarians and other major national sides, with intense relish and commitment.

That has been one of the most attractive ingredients of the Hong Kong event and it surely will be the same at Murrayfield as emergent nations enjoy their moment of glory on the world stage. That David and Goliath element will enhance the World Sevens with the Davids, no doubt, enjoying the bulk of audience support as they seek to topple the heavy artillery.

John Jeffrey and Douglas Morgan have recently been appointed coaches to the Scotland team. The Team Manager of the Murrayfield event will be Charlie Bissett, the former Jordanhill College and Heriot's FP lock who had the distinction of representing three district sides, Glasgow, Edinburgh and, as captain, the North and Midlands. The Team Liaison Co-ordinator is Gordon Dixon (brother of coach Richie Dixon) of Linlithgow, the Referees' Liaison Co-ordinator is Eddie Sheret of Dalkeith, the VIP Liaison Co-ordinators are Sir John Orr and Brigadier Frank Coutts, Gordon Alston will be responsible for the administration side, and Jack Dun of Melrose will give the benefit of his experience as player, first class referee and sevens organiser. They face a huge undertaking for there will be 24 countries represented, each with a squad of ten players and two officials, and there will be some 200 ties with the qualifying event alone

Three Borderers ready for Hong Kong sevens
(*The* Scotsman)

providing some 84 games. To cope with the needs of every squad some 25 liaison officers have been appointed – Alan Quinn, Bill Ure, Colin Hood, Donald Steven, Douglas Lee, Frank Sibbald, Gerry McManus, Iain Forsyth, Jim Robertson, Malcolm Stent, Neville Cross, Peter Millar, Rob Flockhart, Robin Lind, Tom Stratton, Walter Robb, all from Edinburgh, Colin Wells and Jim Chapman from Linlithgow, George Murray from Melrose, Jack Robertson from Grangemouth, John Thorburn from Hawick, Nor-

man Anderson from Kelso, Peter Gallagher from Duns, Sandy Fraser from Stirling and Mike O'Reilly from Penicuik. The training grounds are likely to be Meggetland, Currie, Forrester, Riccarton, Peffermill, Cramond Campus, Fettes Avenue (Lothians and Border Police), Musselburgh, Lismore, Portobello, Royal High School and Murrayfield. The referees' training ground will be Myreside.

The qualifying event placed a genuine 'world' tag on the competition because it provided a step-ladder by which the less-fancied nations could aspire to a place in the Murrayfield finals. The Santa Maria Goretti Stadium in Catania, Sicily, may have seemed an unusual venue for an international sevens qualifying event, especially in the gathering heat of a Sicilian spring, but it was a thrill for the Italian Rugby Federation to host that big event from the 29 to 31 May 1992. Some 17 countries contested the qualifying stage – Namibia, Poland, Portugal, Sweden, Arabian Gulf, Zimbabwe, Hong Kong, Belgium, Morocco, Sri Lanka, Czechoslovakia, Spain, Tunisia, Taiwan, Germany, Malaysia, and Kenya. They were split into two pools of six teams and one of five in which each played the others. The winners and runners-up then formed a new Pool One on the second day and the others were allocated to new Pools Two and Three. Another round robin system was operated on the second day and the teams then ranked one to 17 on the basis of their previous performances, whereupon the top 12 contested the main knock-out competition on day three with the remainder competing for the Plate. It all seems pretty complicated but it worked and it produced

Another strike against England (The Scotsman)

four deserved qualifiers – Namibia, Spain, Taiwan and Hong Kong. The quarter final results by which those four made it to the finals were: Namibia 16 Zimbabwe 10; Spain 12 Portugal 6; Taiwan 20 Sweden 12; Hong Kong 26 Czechoslovakia 6. The success of Namibia in winning the tournament by beating Taiwan, 24–61, in the semi-final and Hong Kong, 26–12 in the final, was in no way surprising when one considers their two victories over Ireland in 1991 and their two narrow defeats by Wales in the fuller version. Namibia played in the Hong Kong sevens for the first time in 1992 and lost to Western Samoa by only 8–0 and everyone knows how formidable those Pacific islanders can be in sevens. Namibia have a prolific try scorer in Gerhard Mans. Hong Kong won their own Plate with a 12–8 extra time win over Tonga. As Hong Kong also reached their own Cup quarter-final for the first time in 1989 it is clear that they will be no pushover at Murrayfield. As for Taiwan they proved the darlings of the crowd at Catania having reached the semi-final of the Plate competition in Hong Kong where they beat Romania by 24–0. The only evidence I personally have seen of Spain in sevens was at the Ulster tournament at Ravenhill, Belfast, in May 1992, when they beat Hawick in extra time – and any side that can do that has to be respected! Of course the Benidorm Sevens in Spain are now well established and acted in 1992 as a preparation tournament prior to the Catania qualifying. Spain also had a squad of 14 on special sevens preparation for Catania which was supervised by their experienced coach, Gerard Murillo. One thing for sure is that those four qualifiers from Catania will

have no problems about lasting the pace at Murrayfield – that is if they have recovered from the testing format that awaited them in the qualifying! There was such a volume of sevens rugby played that, on May 29 for example, play started at 9.30 am and finished at 10.30 pm. The eventual winners faced as many as 12 ties over the three days. It was hot too!

The seven-a-side explosion among the so-called second division nations is attributable in part to the spectacular nature of so much of the action, with cut-and-thrust in thrilling handling passages and only the minimum of time given to the less attractive ball-winning areas. Countries such as Japan and Korea do not possess the physical wherewithal with which to take on the All Blacks, Australia, England and the like on equal terms at fifteens. But sevens lends itself to the enterprise, quick wits, electric handling and sizzling pace of those little men who thus revel in the open spaces with their own distinctive brand of play. Thus at the 1992 Hong Kong event the mighty Barbarians lost in the Cup quarter-final by 16–10 to South Korea, and that in mud and water that one would have thought would have suited the Baa Baas. The big shots will have noticed that both Japan and Korea will be at Murrayfield!

The seven-a-side game continues to spread not least in Australia where two new tournaments were launched successfully in 1991. The Australians will be particularly keen to win the Murrayfield event. For one thing it would give them the World International Sevens title to place alongside the World Cup they won at Twickenham in October 1991. For another, it is a sore point

Black on White. All Blacks devour the Shark (The Scotsman)

with them that, having won the Hong Kong event in 1979, 1982, 1983, 1985 and 1988, and been runners-up in 1981 and 1989, they have failed to make the final in the past three years. Australians like to win. So they established a sevens selection panel comprising their national team coach, Bob Dwyer, John Maxwell, who captained those highly successful Australian sevens of the 70s and 80s and who led the famous Sydney club, Randwick, to their Melrose sevens triumph in 1990, and Roger Gould, full-back in the 'Grand Slam' Wallabies sides which toured the British Isles in 1984.

In the United States there already are some 100 sevens tournaments in a season after which about 30 players are selected to attend a special sevens camp, usually in Phoenix, Arizona in January, from which their US Eagles 1993 sevens squad will be created. Emil Signes, the Eagles sevens coach and manager, who produced a fascinating book on sevens skills and tactics, reckons that the Americans have taken to the sevens game because of its 'athleticism, fluidity, raw flair and pace'.

One of the attractions of sevens too is that there is a place for virtually everyone no matter what shape or size. True enough, selectors do tend to opt for fast forwards who can run and handle and so loose forward types are usually preferred. Yet there is a place for the specialist hooker who can cover the paddock and really big fellows with pace and skill are worth their weight in gold. One of the outstanding personalities to emerge from recent Hong Kong tournaments has been Mesake Rasari of Fiji whose name, through TV and radio coverage, has become

something of a household word. Rasari is 6 ft 5 in and 16 st 11 lb but he can shift too, and one of the most dramatic sights in sevens rugby is when he takes off on one of his thundering gallops. A fearsome sight! In the qualifying tournament in Catania, Namibia's flank forward, Pieter du Plooy, weighed in at 16 st 9 lb. In contrast the Sri Lankan wing, Sudath Sampath, was a mere 9 st 6 lb. There was age contrast too for the Moroccan scrum-half, Rachid Karmouchi, was 36 years old, the Zimbabwean wing, Victor Olonga, just 17.

Rasari is not the only charismatic personality to have been spawned by the abbreviated version. His Fijian colleague, Waisale Serevi, gives the impression of almost having invented the sevens game himself such are his magical qualities. There is that running hitch-kick of his as well as that cheeky overhead, blind pass, followed by Noa Nadruku's between-the-legs delivery that sent Tomasi Cama on the crucial try-scoring run that clinched the 1990 Hong Kong final. Remember also Serevi's delicious little chip ahead and on-the-run collection for another gem of a try against the New Zealanders? Such touches of sparkling genius and unorthodoxy have made the Fijians great crowd favourites and worthy reigning World International Sevens champions.

Fiji will be the team to beat at Murrayfield because not only are they capable of quite startling interplay but they have shown a capacity for adapting to any conditions. At Netherdale in 1991 and at Hong Kong in 1992 they had no problems with filthy weather and treacherous ground conditions. The sevens game is actually more popular in

Fiji than fifteens. Their sevens season extends from October to March so there is vast incentive for those big, dusky Pacific islanders to make the bells ring at Murrayfield by carrying all before them. Of course no side in the tournament will be keener to topple the Fijians than the New Zealanders. They have appeared in eight of the last nine Hong Kong finals and were champions in 1986, 1987 and 1989. But they have not been amused by the fact that, in the last three Hong Kong finals, they have been beaten by Fiji. Such indignity, in New Zealand eyes, only can be erased by them taking the World crown. In the past New Zealand have fielded several gifted and kenspeckle characters such as Frano Botica, John Gallagher and John Schuster (all now Rugby League players), Wayne Shelford and Zinzan Brooke. At the same time they have created sevens personalities out of comparative unknowns such as Eric Rush, who was such a hit with the Barbarians during their centenary games, Pat Lam, who made a big impression in the Western Samoan World Cup squad, Dallas Seymour, who was in the New Zealand squad who won the Students' World Cup in 1988, and Scott Pierce who once scored 11 tries in the 1989 Sydney International Sevens.

One of the most distinctive features of New Zealand sevens strategy has been the unbridled aggression with which they have undertaken their tackling chores. Their engagement of the opponent in possession has been so quick and physical as to prove an intimidatory factor that gives opponents only minimum time on the ball. That has been the Border style, with its up-and-at-'em approach, for over 100 years and it has now been adopted by teams everywhere. Indeed Fiji's recent successes have owed much to the ferocity of their engagement which, when set alongside the unorthodoxy of some of their tackling technique, does tend to create some feeling of apprehension in opposition ranks. So, against Southern hemisphere countries, home countries will have to make intelligent running off the ball a key priority so that the ball can be kept alive. It is harder to stand up in the tackle, and to move the ball away, against opponents who seek to make their tackling a positive weapon of attack.

Whilst it would be in every sense appropriate that Scotland should win the World International Sevens played in the country that gave birth to the sevens game, that assuredly would be some feat having regard to the quality of the opposition, to the fact that of all the glamorous sides from the UK who have competed at the Hong Kong event, including Scotland and Wales as national sides, only the Barbarians have won and that as long ago as 1981, and also that Scotland flattered to deceive when the last World International Sevens were held in Scotland to mark the centenary of the SRU in 1972–73. That tournament was staged at Murrayfield in April 1973. Scotland lost not only to Ireland but also to New Zealand who had little experience of the short game at that time. The results then were: Group A – Scotland 14 Australia 12; Ireland 22 New Zealand 18; Ireland 16 Australia 4; New Zealand 24 Scotland 16; Ireland 24 Scotland 12; New Zealand 16 Australia 12. Group B – England 22 France 0; Wales 30 President's VII 10; England 26 Pres VII 16; Wales 36

*Gary Armstrong against Japan
(World Cup) (The* Scotsman)

Finlay – family man (The Scotsman)

France 4; Pres VII 20 France 16 (extra time); England 24 Wales 10. Final – England 22 Ireland 18. Teams: England – K.J. Fielding, P.S. Preece, P.A. Rossborough and S.J. Smith; F.E. Cotton (capt), J.D. Gray and A.G. Ripley. Ireland – V.E. Becker, J.P. Dennison, A.W. McMaster and C.M.H. Gibson; T.A.P. Moore, D.M. Canniffe and J.F. Slattery. Referee – T.F.E. Grierson (Hawick). Yet Scotland have demonstrated that they are preparing seriously for the World Sevens by taking part in the Selkirk Sevens on 29 August, as well as sending two teams to the Kelso sevens tournament at Poynder Park on 6 September.

In contrast to the straight knockout format that has been in operation in most sevens tournaments ever since that first event at the Greenyards, Melrose, in 1883, whereby sides beaten in the first round play just the one tie the World International Sevens will almost certainly be on a round robin basis that will guarantee a veritable feast of sevens over the three days. In this way each country is guaranteed more than one tie and although all will be aspiring to the top honour, there are those who would derive infinite pleasure from winning a consolation medal.

Each country will be allowed to play any seven players from their squad of ten in any tie so that their choice can change from tie to tie if they so desire. The intention here is to provide the opportunity for every member of each squad to be given a game after, in some cases, having travelled from the other side of the world. The tradition of sevens, of course, from its earliest days, has been for the same seven to play throughout the tournament except in the case of injury. What will be made clear to those taking part is that 'tactical replacements' will not be permitted and that, once a seven takes the field, replacement cannot be made except in the case of genuine injury being verified by the tournament medical officer.

Murrayfield will be a Rugby Union Mecca in April 1993, for the very thought of 24 nations playing in a world sevens tournament including South Africa – and what a thrill it will be to see the famous Springboks at Murrayfield again – is an enthralling prospect and will surely capture the interest of rugby adherents in every corner of the world.

INTERNATIONAL AND CLUB STATISTICS

1991–1992

WORLD CUP 1991 RESULTS

October 5

SCOTLAND 47
SCOTT HASTINGS (*WATSONIANS*) 1T
CRAIG CHALMERS (*MELROSE*) 1T 1P
DEREK WHITE (*LONDON SCOTTISH*) 1T
GAVIN HASTINGS (*WATSONIANS*) 1T 5C 2P
TONY STANGER (*HAWICK*) 1T
FINLAY CALDER (*STEWART'S-MELVILLE FP*) 1T
IWAN TUKALO (*SELKIRK*) 1T

JAPAN 9

October 9

SCOTLAND 52
IWAN TUKALO (*SELKIRK*) 3T
SEAN LINEEN (*BOROUGHMUIR*) 1T
DEREK WHITE (*LONDON SCOTTISH*) 1T
PETER DODS (*GALA*) 5C 2P
DEREK TURNBULL (*HAWICK*) 1T
DODDIE WEIR (*MELROSE*) 1T
DOUG WYLIE (*STEWART'S-MELVILLE FP*) 1DG

ZIMBABWE 12

October 12

SCOTLAND 24
GRAHAM SHIEL (*MELROSE*) 1T
CRAIG CHALMERS (*MELROSE*) 1DG
GARY ARMSTRONG (*JED-FOREST*) 1T
GAVIN HASTINGS (*WATSONIANS*) 2C 3P

IRELAND 15

October 19

SCOTLAND 28
JOHN JEFFREY (*KELSO*) 2T
GAVIN HASTINGS (*WATSONIANS*) 2C 4P
TONY STANGER (*HAWICK*) 1T

WESTERN SAMOA 6

October 26

SCOTLAND 6
GAVIN HASTINGS (*WATSONIANS*) 2P

ENGLAND 9

October 30

SCOTLAND 6
GAVIN HASTINGS (*WATSONIANS*) 2P

NEW ZEALAND 13

5 NATIONS CHAMPIONSHIP

SCOTTISH RESULTS

January 18: Royal Bank of Scotland International

SCOTLAND 7
DEREK WHITE (LONDON SCOTTISH) 1T
GAVIN HASTINGS (*WATSONIANS*) 1P

ENGLAND 25

February 15

SCOTLAND 18
TONY STANGER (*HAWICK*) 1T
ANDY NICOL (*DUNDEE HSFP*) 1T
GAVIN HASTINGS (*WATSONIANS*) 2C 2P

IRELAND 10

March 7: Royal Bank of Scotland International

SCOTLAND 10
NEIL EDWARDS (*HARLEQUINS*) 1T
GAVIN HASTINGS (*WATSONIANS*) 2P

FRANCE 6

March 21

SCOTLAND 12
CRAIG CHALMERS (*MELROSE*) 2P 1DG
GAVIN HASTINGS (*WATSONIANS*) 1P

WALES 15

SUMMARY (*SUNDAY 22 MARCH*)

January 18
SCOTLAND   7   ENGLAND   25

February 15
IRELAND   10   SCOTLAND   18

March 7
SCOTLAND   10   FRANCE   6

March 21
WALES   15   SCOTLAND   12

FINAL TABLE (*SUNDAY 22 MARCH*)

	P	W	D	L	P	A	PTS
ENGLAND	4	4	0	0	118	29	8
FRANCE	4	2	0	2	75	62	4
SCOTLAND	4	2	0	2	47	56	4
WALES	4	2	0	2	40	63	4
IRELAND	4	0	0	4	46	116	0

OTHER INTERNATIONALS

August 31

SCOTLAND 12
IWAN TUKALO (*SELKIRK*) 1T
PETER DODS (*GALA*) 1C 2P

ROMANIA 18

September 16

SCOTLAND 16
KENNY MILNE (*HERIOT'S*) 1T
FINLAY CALDER (*STEWART'S-MELVILLE FP*) 1T
CRAIG CHALMERS (*MELROSE*) 1C 2P

BARBARIANS 16

T   – Tries
C   – Conversions
P   – Penalties
DG– Drop Goals

SCOTLANDS INTERNATIONAL SCORERS

Tries

IWAN TUKALO	(*SELKIRK*)	5
TONY STANGER	(*HAWICK*)	4
DEREK WHITE	(*LONDON SCOTTISH*)	3
FINLAY CALDER	(*STEWART'S-MELVILLE FP*)	2
JOHN JEFFREY	(*KELSO*)	2
KENNY MILNE	(*HERIOT'S*)	1
SCOTT HASTINGS	(*WATSONIANS*)	1
CRAIG CHALMERS	(*MELROSE*)	1

Kicked Points

GAVIN HASTINGS	(*WATSONIANS*)	83
CRAIG CHALMERS	(*MELROSE*)	27
PETER DODS	(*GALA*)	24
DOUG WYLIE	(*STEWART'S-MELVILLE FP*)	3

McEWAN'S DISTRICT MATCHES

14 September 1991

SOUTH	31	GLASGOW	4
EDINBURGH	18	ANGLO SCOTS	12
NORTH AND MIDLANDS	12	PRESIDENTS XV	7

21 September 1991
ANGLO SCOTS	4	PRESIDENTS XV	32
SOUTH	22	EDINBURGH	3
GLASGOW		NORTH AND	
	16	MIDLANDS	3

1 April 1992
| GLASGOW | 16 | EDINBURGH | 12 |

AUSTRALIAN TOUR

28 May 1992
NORTHERN
TERRITORIES
| SELECT | 17 | SCOTLAND | 16 |

31 May 1992
| QUEENSLAND | 15 | SCOTLAND | 15 |

3 June 1992
EMERGING
| WALLABIES | 24 | SCOTLAND | 24 |

6 June 1992
NEW   SOUTH
| WALES | 35 | SCOTLAND | 15 |

9 June 1992
NEW   SOUTH
WALES
| COUNTRY | 10 | SCOTLAND | 26 |

13 June 1992
| AUSTRALIA | 27 | SCOTLAND | 12 |

18 June 1992
QUEENSLAND
COUNTRY
| ORIGIN | 12 | SCOTLAND | 29 |

21 June 1992
| AUSTRALIA | 37 | SCOTLAND | 13 |

McEWAN'S NATIONAL LEAGUE TABLES

DIVISION ONE	P	W	D	L	F	A	PTS
MELROSE	13	11	1	1	263	142	23
EDINBURGH ACADEMICALS	13	10	1	2	266	130	21
HERIOTS FP	13	7	1	5	198	213	15
BOROUGHMUIR	12	6	1	5	210	179	13
GALA	13	6	0	7	237	202	12
SELKIRK	12	6	0	6	228	210	12
WATSONIANS	13	5	2	6	202	185	12
CURRIE	13	6	0	7	231	227	12
JED-FOREST	13	6	0	7	174	173	12
STIRLING COUNTY	13	6	0	7	145	207	12
HAWICK	13	4	2	7	176	193	10
GLASGOW HIGH-KELVINSIDE	13	4	2	7	206	245	10
STEWART'S-MELVILLE FP	13	5	0	8	164	261	10
WEST OF SCOTLAND	13	3	0	10	163	291	6

DIVISION TWO	P	W	D	L	F	A	PTS
KELSO	13	13	0	0	342	116	26
DUNDEE HSFP	11	10	0	1	377	86	20
PEEBLES	13	8	1	4	172	142	17
AYR	13	8	0	5	225	170	16
PRESTON LODGE FP	13	8	0	5	185	216	16
MUSSELBURGH	13	7	0	6	227	192	14
WIGTOWNSHIRE	13	6	1	6	173	170	13
GLASGOW ACADEMICALS	13	5	0	8	190	212	10
EDINBURGH WANDERERS	13	5	0	8	162	225	10
DUNFERMLINE	13	4	1	8	141	230	9
KILMARNOCK	12	4	0	8	103	190	8
KIRKCALDY	12	3	1	8	155	207	7
ROYAL HIGH	13	3	0	10	133	227	6
CORSTORPHINE	13	3	0	10	102	304	6

DIVISION THREE	P	W	D	L	F	A	PTS
GRANGEMOUTH	13	11	1	1	255	130	23
CLARKSTON	13	10	2	1	235	99	22
HADDINGTON	13	9	0	4	201	155	18
HOWE OF FIFE	13	8	0	5	186	206	16
HILLHEAD-JORDANHILL	13	7	1	5	165	143	15
LANGHOLM	13	6	1	6	177	123	13
DUMFRIES	13	5	2	6	184	174	12
BIGGAR	13	5	2	6	164	161	12
HUTCHESON-ALOYSIANS	13	5	1	7	176	175	11
GORDONIANS	13	5	0	8	126	249	10
PORTOBELLO FP	13	4	0	9	152	174	8
PERTHSHIRE	13	3	2	8	161	206	8
TRINITY ACADEMICALS	13	4	0	9	147	224	8
HIGHLAND	13	2	2	9	123	233	6

DIVISION FOUR	P	W	D	L	F	A	PTS
MORGAN ACADEMY FP	13	11	0	2	260	144	22
ST BOSWELLS	13	10	0	3	223	111	202
ALLOA	13	10	0	3	191	124	20
CAMBUSLANG	12	8	0	4	170	113	16
LEITH ACADEMICALS	13	7	1	5	171	149	15
CARTHA QUEENS PARK	13	7	1	5	163	183	15
LINLITHGOW	13	6	0	7	193	180	12
DALZIEL HSFP	12	5	2	5	161	148	12
EAST KILBRIDE	13	5	0	8	140	172	10
EDINBURGH UNIVERSITY	13	5	0	8	143	183	10
ABERDEEN GSFP	13	3	3	7	174	208	9
LISMORE	13	4	0	9	153	226	8
PENICUIK	13	3	1	9	161	244	7
MADRAS COLLEGE FP	13	2	0	11	121	239	4

DIVISION FIVE

	P	W	D	L	F	A	PTS
STEWARTRY	13	12	0	1	302	81	24
LIVINGSTON	13	10	1	2	196	79	21
LENZIE	13	9	0	4	231	89	18
HILLFOOTS	12	7	1	4	143	111	15
PAISLEY	12	7	0	5	184	140	14
GLENROTHES	13	7	0	6	171	131	14
ARDROSSAN ACADEMICALS	13	7	0	6	160	146	14
MORAY	11	6	1	4	142	142	13
NORTH BERWICK	13	6	0	7	178	169	12
FALKIRK	13	5	0	8	166	183	10
WAYSIDERS	13	4	0	9	81	257	8
ABERDEENSHIRE	12	3	1	8	101	232	7
GREENOCK WANDERERS	11	1	0	10	81	212	2
DUNBAR	12	1	0	11	97	261	2

DIVISION SIX

	P	W	D	L	F	A	PTS
CLYDEBANK	13	12	1	0	354	96	25
IRVINE	13	9	1	3	252	77	19
MARR	13	8	1	4	204	122	17
BROUGHTON FP	13	7	1	5	213	102	15
EARLSTON	12	6	3	3	109	101	15
ST ANDREWS UNIVERSITY	12	6	0	6	235	130	12
HARRIS ACADEMY FP	13	5	2	6	147	96	12
LASSWADE	12	5	2	5	182	170	12
MURRAYFIELD	13	5	1	7	142	175	11
DRUMPELLIER	13	5	1	7	166	204	11
CUMBERNAULD	13	5	0	8	126	174	10
FORRESTER FP	13	5	0	8	166	215	10
WALKERBURN	13	3	1	9	128	242	7
CARNOUSTIE HSFP	12	1	0	11	58	578	2

DIVISION SEVEN

	P	W	D	L	F	A	PTS
BERWICK	13	13	0	0	279	56	26
DUNS	12	11	0	1	419	62	22
ROSS HIGH	13	9	0	4	180	131	18
ALLAN GLEN'S	11	7	0	4	202	98	14
PANMURE	13	7	0	6	161	186	14
STIRLING UNIVERSITY	11	6	0	5	118	218	12
GARNOCK	13	5	1	7	171	186	11
RAF KINLOSS	12	5	0	7	185	167	10
MONTROSE	13	5	0	8	122	202	10
WHITECRAIGS	12	5	0	7	127	211	10
STRATHMORE	13	4	1	8	95	235	9
ABERDEEN UNIVERSITY	13	4	0	9	146	207	8
ROSYTH AND DISTRICT	13	3	0	10	102	233	6
CUMNOCK	12	2	0	10	116	231	4